Florida Ghost Stories

Robert R. Jones

Pineapple Press, Inc.
Sarasota, Florida

This book is dedicated to Muffin,
a faithful friend and companion for many years.

Inquiries should be addressed to:

Pineapple Press, Inc.
P.O. Box 3889
Sarasota, Florida 34230

www.pineapplepress.com

Library of Congress Cataloging-in-Publication Data

Jones, Robert R.
  Florida ghost stories / Robert R. Jones. — 1st ed.
     p. cm.
  Includes index.
  ISBN 978-1-56164-411-7 (pbk. : alk. paper)
  1. Ghosts—Florida. I. Title. BF1472.U6J67 2007
  133.109759—dc22
                                        2007041018
First Edition
10 9 8 7 6 5 4 3 2 1

Design by Shé Heaton
Printed in the United States of America

Contents

Acknowledgments

I would like to thank my wife, Dottie, for the help and encouragement she has continued to give me. Without her help in proofing and typing, and without her suggestions, this book would most likely still be undone.

This book is for all of you who like the old stories that were told around a campfire or in the living room on a stormy night when the lights would go out, and to those of you who just like an old story without the horror and gore that we see so much of nowadays at the movies and on television.

Preface

The following stories are of ghosts, spirits, and tall tales of strange events that have, or may have taken place in this area of Florida over the past three hundred years. You must be the judge as to their truth or not. Some have been told to me as truths.

There are some definitions according to the eleventh edition of Merriam-Webster's Collegiate Dictionary:

Ghost 1: the seat of life or intelligence: soul 2: a disembodied soul, esp. the soul of a dead person believed to be an inhabitant of the unseen world or to appear to the living in bodily likeness 3: spirit, demon.

Spirit 1: an animating or vital principle held to give life to physical organisms. 2: a supernatural being or essence as a: Holy Spirit. b: soul. c: an often malevolent being that is bodiless but can become visible specifically. d: a malevolent being that enters and possesses a human being.

Specter or Spectre 1: a visible disembodied spirit: ghost. 2: something that haunts or perturbs the mind; phantasm.

Poltergeist a noisy usually mischievous ghost held to be responsible for unexplained noises (as rapping).

Curse a prayer on invocation for harm or injury to come upon one.

Site Map

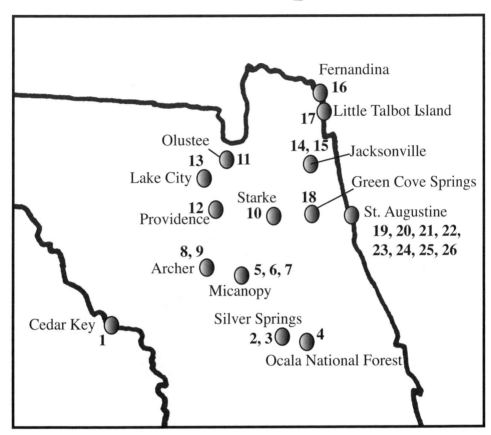

Fernandina
16

17 Little Talbot Island

Olustee
13 **11**

Lake City

14, 15 Jacksonville

Green Cove Springs

Starke **18**

12 **10** St. Augustine
Providence **19, 20, 21, 22,**
23, 24, 25, 26

8, 9
Archer **5, 6, 7**
Micanopy

Silver Springs

Cedar Key **2, 3** **4**
1 Ocala National Forest

1

Rosewood

Cedar Key

This story was told to me many years ago. It must have been around 1958, or close to it. My friends Ralph and Michael were going fishing at Cedar Key, Florida. The morning was warm but very foggy. They had left early that morning, not only to get an early start, but also to purchase bait for their fishing trip. After passing through Archer on their way to Cedar Key, they decided to stop for breakfast at one of the quaint little restaurants in Cedar Key. The food had always been good any time they stopped.

I will try to tell the story as Ralph told it to me. He and Michael had driven a good ways from Archer and knew that they should be getting close to their destination. When all of a sudden *Bang! Bump! Bump! Bump!* went the old car. Ralph said, "I guess I had better pull over, sounds as if we have a flat tire." He pulled over to the side of the road and sure enough, they had a flat. Michael mumbled a few unintelligible words about the old tire as he was getting the spare out of the trunk.

They had just finished changing the tire when they heard noises coming from their right, off in the woods. It sounded like gunshots, then screaming and all kinds of yelling. They knew that it couldn't be hunters, because they never made that much commotion—even the

drunks down in Gulf Hammock. They started to walk up the old dirt road. Just a little way up the road they saw a sign that read "Rosewood."

"Never heard of the place," Ralph said.

"I haven't either," replied Michael.

Then, seemingly out of nowhere, from the fog came a black man. When he saw them, he stopped dead in his tracks and fell to his knees crying and begging. "Please, misters, don't kill me. I didn't do it. None of us did. Oh, Lord! Please believe me."

They looked him over for a moment. He had been beaten badly about the face and head. His eyes were puffy and blood was running from his nose and right ear. They could see a deep gash on the left side of his head and rope burns on his wrists.

Michael said to him, "Don't worry. We aren't going to hurt you. What's going on over there anyway? We can hear the gunshots and screaming. Who's doing it?"

"Oh, misters! You got to get us help. Those white folks are beating and killing every colored. They are catching men, women, and children. You got to help!"

"Why are they doing this?" Ralph asked.

"They thinks one of us coloreds raped and beat up a white woman. But we didn't do it, sir. Lord knows we didn't, we didn't! They ain't listening to nobody."

"How do you know the coloreds didn't do it?"

Very calmly he looked Ralph straight in the eye and said, "I knows because I saw the man that done it. That's why some of them wants me dead."

"Well, you go get in the back of the car. We'll take you with us to Cedar Key and you can tell your story to the police there."

"They'll kill me for sure, mister."

"No, they won't. We'll see to that. What's your name anyway?"

"My name's James, sir. James Washington. I do want to thank you, misters."

They drove on into Cedar Key, and as they came to the first little country store, they stopped because there was a police car parked in front. They went inside and saw the policeman standing at the counter drinking a cup of coffee. He turned to them and said, "You men going fishing? It's been really good this past few days."

"Yes, sir, but we've got a little problem."

"Oh? What's the problem?"

They told him what James had said about what had happened in Rosewood.

"Well, where is this James Washington?"

"He's in the back seat of the car out front."

"I think I should go and have a little talk with this James."

They followed him out the door. As they walked toward the car, the policeman asked where they were from. Michael told him Jacksonville, and they were on their way fishing.

The policeman opened the car door and looked in, then turned back to them, looking a little angry.

"Are you fellows trying to pull one on me? There isn't anyone in that back seat."

They looked in. James was gone, but there was blood on the door and window. "He was here. Look at the blood he left on the window glass. Someone had to lean on it," they said.

"Well boys, I think you had better go on your fishing trip and forget about this."

"Why? We heard gunshots and the screams before James came up."

"Now look, boys, are you really sure that you have never heard of Rosewood?"

"Yes, sir, we're sure."

"You boys come on inside and have a cup of coffee with me and I'll tell you about Rosewood."

They got their cups of coffee and listened to the story as the policeman told it.

"Now, you see, many years ago, Rosewood was a colored settlement until nineteen-twenty-four, when it happened. There were a few white families that worked in the lumber mills and turpentine stills, but mostly it was colored. The story goes that one of the young black men that lived in Rosewood knew this white woman was alone after her husband went to work at the sawmill. The whites assumed he just snuck in the house and raped her. When she got away and told her story, all hell broke loose. The Klan and white men from all around this area tore loose on the settlement. They did kill some coloreds, I'm sure, and they burned every colored's house there."

"But if you knew this was happening, why didn't you do something about it?"

"I couldn't."

"Why?"

"Because as I told you, Rosewood was destroyed in nineteen-twenty-four, more than thirty years ago."

"That can't be," they told him. "We heard it!"

"I'm sure you did. You are not the first I've heard tell the story about the sounds, and a few have even met James. You see, James was the colored they believed done the raping. After it was all over James was never found. We believe he was caught and killed by the mob. Don't know why he keeps coming back."

"Maybe he really didn't do the rape as they thought."

"That could be true. Many claimed that it wasn't a black man at all, but a white man traveling through. I guess old James won't be at rest until justice is done."

A few days after hearing Ralph and Michael's story, I asked my Dad if he knew anything about Rosewood. He was a young man at that time living in Archer, a small town close by.

"Yes, son, I know about Rosewood. I was there."

"Tell me about it," I said.

"It was a terrible thing. No one talked about it much. I went over with my Papa. At the time, we thought we were going to help track down the man that did it. When we got there, things had already gotten out of hand. My Papa was a strong man, but a fair man. When he saw all the burning and killing, he told me we were going home. Some of the other men tried to shame him for not taking part, but they knew better than to push him too far. Even if they were drunk, he wouldn't take anything like that from any man. He was a blacksmith in Maddox Foundry and they all knew he could back it up."

"Did they ever catch the man that did it?"

"I don't think so, son. For years after no one would talk about it. I believe old James is trying to find someone to help him get justice for what happened that night, and someday I'm sure he will."

Epilogue

In 1990 the Florida Legislature awarded compensation to some of the survivors and their descendants for the lands they had lost in Rosewood.

2

Mourning Dove and Running Fox

Silver Springs

There are many tales told about the ancient Indians who lived in Florida many years ago, long before the white man came to Florida. One story is about a beautiful Indian maiden. Some of the tales about her say she was a princess from one of the northern tribes, but wherever she may have come from, most of the eastern tribes say basically the same thing about her. Even some of the names given her were similar.

Here in Florida, her name was Mourning Dove. No one knows exactly to what tribe she belonged. They only tell that she came down from the north with her family's people to the great Peace Camp that was held approximately very four years.

As the story goes, they had traveled many days from their home before they arrived in Florida (or, as it was called by the Indians, "Land of Plenty"). They took their war canoes into the great river that flowed into the sea, then went south for many days until they came to the crystal waters that would lead them to the great campgrounds.

Every four years or so, many Indian tribes would meet on the banks of Crystal Springs. Some called it Blue Run and today it is known as Silver Springs. All the Indian tribes met there in peace. Many could have been mighty enemies at other times, but here there were no wars or fights. Many games were held, not un-like the Olympic games in Greece. All their differences were put aside for the weeks of games and peace.

We are told that Mourning Dove was the most beautiful of all the Indian maidens. The braves of all the tribes were trying to gain her favor, but she had not shown any interest in any of them until one day she was out sitting by the river on an old crooked palm tree watching as the water games were played. The water was so clear that she could sit there and see everything, even what was going on under water. All of a sudden, from out of nowhere, she was roughly pushed into the water.

Down, down she went into the cold, clear water. She came up, angry at whoever could have done such a thing. When she pulled herself from the water, she saw a very handsome Seminole standing there with his hand out to help her out of the water.

Very angrily she said, "I have never been treated so badly in my life. Why did you do such a thing as push me into the water?"

He smiled down at her and said, "Your life is now mine, beautiful princess."

"How do you think you have a right to say that to me?"

"Because I have just saved your life, so by our laws, your life now belongs to me," he replied.

Looking around her, then back at him she said, "How did you save my life? I see no danger here."

"Come with me and I will show you."

She took his hand and he pulled her up and led her to the tree where she had been sitting. Then he pointed to the spot where she had been only moments before.

Her eyes followed to the spot he was pointing. There, stuck into the tree, was a huge cottonmouth moccasin with a knife through its head. She knew at once that if this snake had bitten her, she would have died.

Then the Seminole spoke. "I was walking by and saw you sitting there in that tree when the snake came. It was about to strike as you became excited over the games. I didn't have time to warn you and I was afraid that I couldn't get to him fast enough, so I pushed you out of the way and stabbed him with my knife."

Mourning Dove smiled at him. "So that's why I went for a swim. What's your name?"

He smiled back at her and said, "My people call me Running Fox."

"Well, Running Fox, would you come to my family's lodge tonight and eat with us? My father would like to meet you, I'm sure."

"I would be honored to have supper with the beautiful Mourning Dove."

She smiled again and told him that she would look for him.

When she got back to her father's lodge, Mourning Dove told her father about the handsome Running Fox and how he had saved her life. Her father, Big Bear, had heard of him.

"I hear that he is the swiftest runner here. I am also told that everyone eats the dust from his feet."

That night as they ate, Big Bear told the rest of his people how Mourning Dove had been saved. He also told them that Running Fox was to be made welcome at his lodge any time.

Over the next few weeks, Mourning Dove and Running Fox were seen together everywhere. It was obvious to all that at last the beautiful Mourning Dove was in love and everyone expected them to announce their marriage soon. Everyone seemed very happy for them and accepted Running Fox as well.

That is, everyone except Brown Dog. He had been in love with Mourning Dove, but she had shown no interest in him. Then, in the cross-country foot race, Running Fox had beaten him badly. He felt that he had lost face with the other tribes.

Brown Dog felt that he could stand it no more, so late one afternoon, he lay waiting for Running Fox by the path he knew Running Fox must follow back to his lodge. Brown Dog picked up a large stone and waited. He hadn't been there long when he heard Running Fox coming. As Running Fox passed, Brown Dog rose and hit him hard in the head with the stone.

Later that night, Running Fox's people found him lying in the path unconscious and took him back to his tent. Then they sent word to Mourning Dove to come because they were sure that he would be dead before morning.

When she arrived, Running Fox awoke just long enough to see her wiping his face, tears running down her cheeks. Then he spoke.

"Mourning Dove, my dear Mourning Dove, don't cry for me. I die happy because I had your love for even this short time. Brown Dog may have killed me, but our love will live on. From this day forth, I cast my spell on any couple who meet and fall in love inside the arms of our old palm. If they do, their love will last forever."

She leaned over and kissed him as he died. Running Fox was wrapped and weighted, then his body was dropped into the deepest part of the springs. Some even today say that it has no bottom.

Now Mourning Dove was shattered with grief. She stood up in her dugout and spoke to the others. "I must add one more enchantment. From this day, anyone who takes two flowers from the underwater grass and places one in each shoe will soon find love. If they take one flower and place it in their right shoe, they will rid themselves of someone who is causing them trouble."

She turned, reached down for the vine that held a large stone used as an anchor, wrapped it around her neck and said, "I now go to be with Running Fox. He is waiting for me." Then she jumped over the side.

Everyone could see her as she followed his body into the deep hole at the bottom of the spring. It was narrow and she was soon gone from sight. Then, to everyone's amazement, a very strange thing happened. No sooner had Mourning Dove disappeared from their sight into the hole than a beautiful spray of white lime rock burst forth from it, as if the springs were saying, "I have these lovers now. They will be happy together forever."

To this day you can still see the white lime rock coming from that spot.

No one seems to know for sure what happened to Brown Dog. Some say Running Fox's family killed him. Others say the gators got him. Still other tales say he is still out there, doomed for eternity to wander the swamps, never to find true love and peace until he does just the right deed helping others who have problems with their love.

Many stories are told of the enchantments Mourning Dove placed on the underwater flowers and many people insist that the stories are true. People also tell of Running Fox's enchantment on the old palm tree by the springs, insisting that they, too, are true.

On your next trip to Silver Springs, look for the enchanted tree and for the underwater snowfall, as some call it. The guides sometimes call it "The Bridal Chamber." The lime rock still bursts forth and marks the spot where Mourning Dove and Running Fox are together and happy.

All the Indians are gone now, except for a few who come now and then to see their ancestors' old Peace Camp. They also come to retell the tale about the two lovers and to see the place where love will never die.

Remember, if you are having problems with a love of your own and out of nowhere an old ragged Indian should come out and offer his help, listen to him. He may be able to help you, and better yet, you may be the one who is destined to give him his final peace by being the right one to help remove the curse on him.

3

Brown Dog's Curse

Silver Springs

This story has been told in many different forms around central Florida and especially the swamps and woods near what is now Silver Springs. You see, many years before it was called Silver Springs, it was called Fort King on the Crystal Springs, and many years before that it was called the Peace Camp by many Indian tribes. This was a place where the tribes would meet and compete with one another in sports, much like people in Ancient Greece did during the Olympic games. All wars and fighting would stop.

The story I am about to tell takes place around the 1890s. My grandfather told it to me many times and always swore that it was true. As he got older and was put into a nursing home, he would get very angry if anyone said that they didn't believe his story.

Grandpa was a young man back then, in his early twenties. I will try to tell the story as he told it to me so long ago.

At the mouth of the Ocklawaha River was a big resort where many tourists would come to spend their winters. The resort was also the site of old Fort King back during the Indian Wars. The tourists would take the riverboats (small like the old paddle-wheelers on the Mississippi). They would board the boats in Jacksonville and travel up the St. Johns River, across Lake George, then up the Ocklawaha River to Fort King

and Ocala. In many places, the river was just barely wide enough for the boat to get through; in others it was very wide. The water was crystal clear all up the river. Many passengers would stand on the upper decks and take shots at an alligator sunning himself on a nearby sandbank. Many times, as the boat would round the bend, it would almost run down an old Florida Cracker out fishing, who would scramble out of the way in his old boat as he shook his fist at the river captain.

On one trip in the early fall, we were making good time up the old river even though a heavy fog had begun to come in. With each passing minute, the visibility diminished. The captain and I had become pretty good friends, and I was by his side in the wheelhouse. Most of the passengers had gone below because the fog had gotten so thick they couldn't see anything anyway.

As I said, most passengers had gone below except for a young couple on their way to Fort King to be married. Everyone on the boat could tell how very much in love they were just by looking at them. They were standing on the upper deck with their arms around each other. We knew they really didn't care if we could see or not. They were only interested in each other.

As we were coming up on Dead Man's Bend, I told the captain we should slow down a bit, just in case there was another old Cracker or something around the bend. He slowed our boat down as we rounded the bend.

Then we heard a blood-chilling sound. Just around the bend was another riverboat. We knew we couldn't avoid hitting it. There was a mighty crash and our whole boat shook. We heard a woman's scream and immediately after that a cry for help. I knew at once what had happened. I ran onto the deck where the young man was standing looking down at the water. I will never forget the look of complete and absolute horror on his face. He pointed down at the water, but could only say, "I can't swim. Help her, please! Someone, for God's sake, help her!"

I looked over the rail and saw her go under the paddle wheel. Without thinking, I dove over the side to help her. I swam around the back of the boat and dove under. About that time I saw something white in front of me. I reached out and grabbed it. It was the shawl she had been wearing on the deck. I looked farther ahead and saw what appeared to be two people—the girl and a man I didn't recognize—swimming downriver. I swam after them, but the current was too strong. I searched a bit longer, then gave up. The girl and whoever the man was must have drowned.

I swam back to the boat and was helped aboard. The young man ran up to me crying, "Did you find her?"

I handed him the shawl. He looked at it, then looked pleadingly at me, begging me to give him some kind of encouragement with my eyes. Then, pulling the shawl to his face, he broke down. Repeating over and over, he said, "Oh Lord, please don't take her from me! I love her so."

We took one of the dinghies and searched down the river for her without success while the men repaired our boat. Several hours later, we were again on our way to Fort King. For the next two days, the young man stood by the rails, just looking out with tears running down his face.

When we docked at the Fort King Landing, all of the other passengers left the ship. I had wondered these last few days about what I had seen in the water. I could have sworn I saw two people, but no one except the girl had been reported missing.

The young man, the captain, and I were the last to leave. We had to make a report of the accident and the missing girl.

As we entered the police chief's office, we noticed a commotion coming from the back room, sounding like women's voices. We told the chief what had happened and where it had taken place. Then he asked, "What was the girl wearing? Describe her to me."

The young man told him that she was wearing a pink dress with lots of ruffles and lace. Her hair was a dark auburn and when she let it down, it reached far below her waist.

The chief looked stunned for a moment, then said, "Will you men follow me? I want you to see something."

We were led through the door into the back room. Our mouths dropped open. For there, standing in the middle of the room, was our missing girl. Her dress was dirty and torn and her hair was down, but it was her. She and her young man flew into each other's arms. They held each other for some time with tears running down their cheeks.

The captain and I were astonished, to say the least, because we couldn't understand how she could have possibly gotten to Fort King before we did. It was upstream against the currents from Dead Man's Bend where she fell into the river. Later she told us her amazing story:

"I remember falling over the rails of the boat and hitting the water. I didn't feel hurt, but I could feel the weight of my wet clothes pulling me under. I pulled my shawl off and tried to get my skirts off. Just as I got them off, everything seemed to go dark. I must have passed out from lack of air. Then, from what seemed like way off somewhere, I heard someone say, 'Hold on, I'm coming.' Out of nowhere I felt a hand touch me and grab my waist. I felt whoever it was pulling me through the water.

"The next thing I can remember was waking up. I was lying on the ground wrapped in a blanket. All of my clothes were draped over the nearby bushes. Except for the blanket, I was completely naked. From behind another tree, I saw the Indian. He had a very kind manner. I didn't feel a bit afraid or ashamed of my nakedness in front of him as he helped me dress.

"He then fixed some soup and told me to drink it for my strength. I did as he suggested, then he led me to Silver Springs. He said that we would make better time on land. When we came to a clearing next to that old curled palm tree, he said that he could go no further. I asked him his name and thanked him for all he had done. All he said was that I had done him a good deed. Now he could rest in peace. I turned back around to ask him what he meant by that and to tell him that you would reward him, but he was gone. I called and called, but he never came. About that time, the police chief's wife heard me and came to help."

Then the police chief asked her, "What was the Indian's name?"

"He said that his name was Brown Dog," she replied.

The police chief and the riverboat captain looked at each other in astonishment and disbelief.

Later that night at supper, the police chief told me the story of Brown Dog, Mourning Dove, and Running Fox, of how a curse was put on Brown Dog for killing Running Fox.

When he had ended the story, the chief said, "Maybe this will be the end of the curse placed on Brown Dog so many years ago."

It has now been over a hundred years since my grandfather was on that riverboat that fateful night, but I believe Brown Dog is now truly at rest because no one has reported any further contact with him. The curse has at last been lifted.

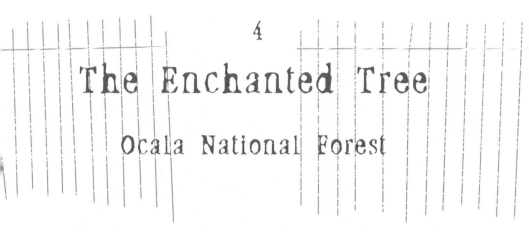

4

The Enchanted Tree

Ocala National Forest

For many years there has been a legend in north central Florida of an enchanted tree. This tree is a live oak that covers a very large area. The limbs of the tree close to the ground are bigger than most trees in the area. This tree is said to be the home of many wild animals that live in the forest, from the smallest hummingbirds to the biggest Florida panthers and black bears.

As the story goes, way back in Florida history, even before the Spanish came, a Seminole chief named Panther put an enchantment on the tree and a curse on the area around it. The chief and his people loved all the animals that lived there. The animals stayed close to these Indians because they trusted them. This Indian tribe and the animals had lived together in peace and happiness for many years. Their children played with the panthers and bears without fear. Then one day while Chief Panther and his people were out foraging for foods like swamp cabbage, wild grapes, plums, and different kinds of berries, another Indian tribe known as the Cherokees, who were from up north in Georgia, came through the area and camped nearby. They were amazed at all the different kinds of wildlife that were around.

This tribe of Indians started to kill the animals. It didn't matter to them how many they killed or why. They killed everything in sight,

19

whether they were needed for food or clothing or not.

A few days later, Chief Panther and his people returned. As they came closer to their campsite near the Great Tree, he saw fewer animals than usual. By this time, the animals should be all around since they always came out to greet the tribe when they returned. But this time, none of them came. When Chief Panther got to the tree, there at its base was a dead female deer with her baby standing beside her. On the other side of the tree was a dead bear, and many dead birds and other animals. With tears in his eyes, he went back to the dead deer and found an arrow in her side where she had been shot. The good chief took the baby up in his arms and gave it to some of the women to look after and protect.

The chief then took some of his men and started out after the other Indians to talk to them about this unnecessary killing of the wild animals in this area of the forest. The next day, they had followed the trail of the other Indians, and by about noon had them in sight. As they approached the clearing coming through the high savanna reeds, an arrow came out of the reeds and hit Chief Panther in the chest. His men ran to him to see if they could help, but they immediately saw that it was a fatal blow. Their beloved chief was dying. About that time, two Indian boys came running through the reeds and when they saw the chief lying on the ground dying, they turned and ran back to their camp.

It wasn't long before the boys' leaders came. They saw what had happened and were very sorry. They said that the boys were young and had thought it was a deer and had never meant to harm anyone.

Chief Panther asked to be propped up so he could speak to them. He said, "My tribe has lived in harmony and closeness with the animals for many years. We have never killed for fun or pleasure. We know that most tribes do kill for food, and we have no problem with this. But I cannot understand killing only for sport. From now on, I place a curse on this area. No animal can be killed within sight of the Great Live Oak Tree, and if any should try, as punishment they will not be able to kill anything for one year. Their arrows will not hit their marks. They will be forced to eat roots, plants, and berries for that year to make them remember this senseless killing of the animals. The Great Oak will be enchanted and will be a haven for all animals that are being killed for no good reason. Other animals who may be near to this Great Oak shall also be protected."

With this last curse, Chief Panther died. He was taken back to the corner of the Great Oak, where his burial mound was built. The tribe of Cherokees worked alongside the Seminoles to help build it. All animals that were left in the area came to Chief Panther's burial, as though they knew that they were safe. The Great Oak was filled with all types of birds. At the edge of the clearing stood deer, bears, panthers, and all kinds of animals, all to pay their respects to Chief Panther one more time.

The tribe of Cherokees decided it was time to go back north to their homes. When they returned to their camps to gather their belongings, though, all their food, skins, and feathers from the animals they had killed had been destroyed by fire. It seems that while they were gone, lightning hit some dry brush close by and burned everything. Everyone knew that it was the start of old Chief Panther's curse and enchantment of his tree. The Seminoles helped them get roots and plants to eat on their way back north.

As the story is told, old Chief Panther's tribe stayed in the area for many years until the white man came, then they moved further south to the Big Cypress in the Everglades.

Not much more is told of the Indians and the Great Oak. Most of them know the curse and enchanted tree and would not go near it, much less hunt close to it, for fear that they may make a mistake and become victims of Chief Panther's curse.

There is a story of some trappers who ventured into the area. They had heard of the old Indian legend and tales of the enchanted tree and the curse of Chief Panther. Most trappers during that time thought nothing about it, and these men were no different.

The trappers followed some tracks, which were getting fresher, and they knew that it wouldn't be long before they found them. As they came into the clearing, there in the middle, standing under a huge oak tree, were six big beautiful deer. As they were quite close, they knew there was no way they could miss and both trappers fired in unison. They didn't see any deer fall, but they knew it wasn't unusual for a deer to run a little way before it fell. They were certain the deer would be on the other side of the tree, so they ran around it. As they came around the tree, there were no deer, but standing in front of them, no more than fifteen feet away, was the biggest black bear they had ever seen. He stood up on his hind legs and started toward them. They both reloaded their muskets and fired at point-blank range but the bear kept coming, as though the bullets had passed right through him. They threw their knives at him and watched as they passed through the big bear. The two trappers were so frightened that they turned and started to run, but there directly in front of them at the edge of the clearing were two big and ferocious panthers. They were so terrified they couldn't run. They had no weapons left, so they just knelt down where they were and prayed, knowing that at any moment they would be killed and eaten. They kept their heads down and their eyes closed, not wanting to see what was coming. After what seemed to be a very long time, they looked up. The panthers were gone and so was the big bear. They slowly got up, picked up their weapons, and started back to their camp. As they left, they could see that the big oak was filled with wild animals, all of whom seemed to be laughing at them.

When they got back to camp, they told their story. One of the old Spaniards said, "You were at the Enchanted Tree, and old Chief Panther's curse got you."

They shook their heads in disbelief. Then the Spaniard brought out a mirror. "Look at yourselves."

When they looked into the mirror, they saw that their hair and beards had turned completely gray. There was no doubt in their minds now that it had indeed been the curse.

There is another story about the Enchanted Tree that is not so frightening. It's about a little girl of about four or five who was camping with her mother and father. They weren't hunting with anything but a camera. At some point the little girl wandered off into the forest alone. Later, when her parents discovered she was missing, they became frantic. They called and hunted all day looking for the little girl. It started to get a bit cold and dark, too cold for the little girl to be in the forest alone. They knew it was too far back to the ranger's station, so they continued their search for her all night.

Early the next morning, they came into the clearing. There in the middle of it was a great oak tree, and under the tree was their little girl. She was sound asleep. She was covered with leaves, feathers, and very soft hair, almost as though it had been placed around her. Next to her was a small pile of berries and grapes. They ran to her and woke her up. All she would say was, "Where are the animals, Daddy?"

He looked around; all he could see were some birds and a few chattering squirrels in the big oak tree. Later that day, as they talked, the little girl told them the strangest story about how the bears had taken her to the tree and made her a bed. She told them that she was hungry and the rabbits and squirrels brought her some berries to eat. The bears stayed with her all night to keep her warm. They told her that they would help her find her parents the next day.

When the family got back to the ranger's cabin, they told him what had happened. He then told them the legend of the Enchanted Oak Tree and the curse of the forest. They had never heard of it before. Every year after that, though, they would take food and place it in the woods for the animals. They never could find that same old tree again.

There have been many stories of hunters and trappers over the years who have made the mistake of killing for no good reason. Some have come upon the Enchanted Tree and fallen under the curse, never to forget their experience. It leaves a mark on them forever.

If you are in the forest and are not doing anything wrong, such as killing for no good reason, and you come to the Great Oak, you will have no problems. You can take pictures and truly have a wonderful time with the animals. The tree is always full. But woe unto the man, woman, or child who mistreats any animals.

No one has ever been able to tell exactly where this tree is located. We do know that it is somewhere in north central Florida. I have often wondered if it truly is one great oak or many oaks. Whatever it is, if I were in the area, I would always be kind to all animals, mainly because I love to see them running free and happy. But you never know when you may come upon the Enchanted Tree, or fall under the curse of old Chief Panther.

5

Herlong Mansion

Micanopy

This is the story of the ghost of Herlong Mansion in Micanopy, Florida. Micanopy is about twelve miles south of Gainesville, in the middle of the state. It is also listed as the second-oldest continuously occupied city in the United States and is named after a Seminole chief. This was originally an Indian town way before the white man came.

It is believed that the original house was built somewhere around the 1840s, right after the Seminoles were either sent to Oklahoma or driven further south to the Everglades. Around the turn of the century, it was refurbished and made into a beautiful two-story brick mansion, using the original structure as a base. This was done by old Mr. Herlong, who owned a large lumber mill and other properties in the area.

As the story goes, many people have seen strange lights coming from the upstairs windows and the attic windows late at night. If you should stay at the mansion, which is now a very fine bed and breakfast, the current owner and manager will not tell you about the ghost until the morning breakfast. He says he wouldn't want his guests to leave during the night if they should hear any strange sounds or see anything unusual there.

Some of the stories about the ghost of Herlong Mansion are from

when the current owner was cleaning the place up and having it repainted. The workmen would come in sometimes and find that their things had been strewn about. They would also be frightened by strange and unexplained sounds coming from the walls and other places. Some of the bravest of them even tried to stay all night. They would hear and feel strange things, but never saw anything. The attic has never been finished; the current owner says that he hopes to make it his apartment someday if he can find workers that will stay on the job.

One of the owner's favorite stories about the house is about his own son. It seems that his son has been a practical joker ever since he was a little fellow. The owner was getting an unusual number of calls from people in town about sightings of strange lights and faces in the attic windows late at night. He would go up to check, but he never saw anything unusual. Then one night as he was sitting in the kitchen having a cup of coffee and getting things ready for breakfast, he heard a terrible scream coming from the attic. He ran up the stairs as fast as he could. As he reached the second floor, his son burst out of the door that led to the attic rooms. His face was as white as a sheet and he was shaking so hard it took almost twenty minutes for him to calm down enough to tell his father what had happened.

After a while, when he had calmed down enough to tell his father what had happened, the boy told his father that he had been going up there late at night with a flashlight. He would stand at the window and hold the light under his chin, which gave him a very eerie look from the street below. However, this night, as he was standing at the window with the light, he felt something touch his arm. Thinking that his dad had found him out, he turned around. But there, only a few feet from him, stood a woman dressed in a long, white dress that reached the floor. She had a shawl over her shoulders. She was translucent; you could see her in every detail, yet you could see right through her. This apparition didn't say a word. She just stood there with a stern look on her face pointing her finger at him. He screamed, dropped his flashlight, and ran out of the attic as fast as possible. He and his father went back up there later to see if they could see anything, but all they found was the flashlight, still shining right where he had dropped it.

After that night, all of the boy's practical jokes were over. He would have nothing to do with the attic; in fact, to this day, he won't stay in the house more than is absolutely necessary.

There have been many sightings and many speculations as to what the ghost is and why it is there. One is that a young, beautiful girl is still waiting for her lover to return from the Civil War. He was killed in the Battle of Chattanooga, but she still lights a candle for him every night to help him find his way home. But none of the old folks in the area know anything about that, or who she may have been.

While we were checking for causes of some of the strange and unusual noises in and around the house, one v

found. When some of the men were explorir

came across a room in the middle of the olu

about ten feet by twelve feet, with no doors and only

men climbed down into the room and found nothing bu .

room. They have checked with all of the old families in the area a.

no one knew anything about this room, or even that it existed. Some

did have some pretty good theories about it, though.

When old Mr. Herlong's son was small, he played all over the house, but he doesn't remember anything about the room. When asked about it, though, he said that before the Civil War, the people who owned the original wood frame house were part of the Underground Railroad that helped slaves escape. He suggested that this room was probably where the escaped slaves were kept until they could get away.

Others say that it was probably used to store moonshine during the Prohibition era of the 1920s. However, Mr. Herlong's son was living in the house then and doubts that theory. His father never drank and he didn't care for those who did. He would not allow alcohol in the house at all.

Maybe we will never know the true answers about the room without a door that is located under this old house and seems to have no purpose or use in the construction of it, and maybe we will never know for sure who this ghostly woman is or why she haunts the house. We do know that she has been seen by many people and is always described the same way. We also know that the earliest recorded mention of her was in 1875 in some old letters, but no mention of the room has been found.

So if you should stay at the Herlong Mansion, don't be afraid if you hear weird sounds or see a lady in a long, white dress pass you ectedly. There is no record of her causing harm to anyone. She always been friendly. And the hospitality at the Herlong Mansion worth the trip.

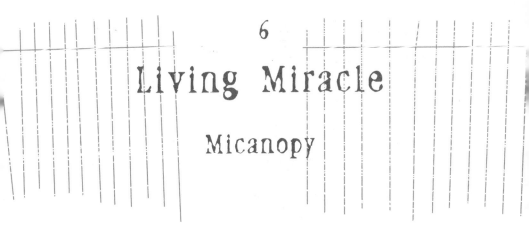

6

Living Miracle

Micanopy

As strange as it may seem, my mother, Lois Zetrouer Jones, died when she was eight years old. She was born on May 6, 1905, and pronounced dead by the town doctor eight years later in July 1913. The details of her death were told to her by her grandmother, who raised her along with her younger sister. It happened this way.

Just before school let out for the summer of 1913, Lois's class was to perform a play that the students had been practicing for some time. Lois had the part of a little red hen and was very excited about it. But on the day of the performance, she came down with a high fever and was sent home with what was later diagnosed as typhoid fever.

Her fever continued to rise and Lois drifted in and out of consciousness for the next few weeks. During that time, her mother and older sister came down with typhoid and died within a week of each other, but Lois lingered on. The doctor told Lois's grandmother to be prepared for the worst because Lois had been much sicker than either her mother or her sister. He didn't expect her to live much longer.

Several days later the doctor came by to check on her condition and found that Lois had stopped breathing. He checked her vital signs and could not detect a heartbeat. Lois was pronounced dead.

Her grandmother went into the nearby town of Micanopy to pur-

Lois at age 89 looking at her tombstone

chase a new dress and casket for Lois to be buried in. As was the custom in those days, her grandmother sent a messenger around town to announce the death and date of the funeral. She also had a tombstone put up with their names on it.

The nurse, who had helped care for Lois during her sickness, now dressed her for burial, placed her in the casket, and set it up in the parlor of the family's home.

Meanwhile Granny had made soup and asked the maid to carry some into the nurse. Many people were afraid to be around the dead and their family maid was no exception.

"Mrs. Hunt," the maid said, "I just don't like going in there with little Miss Lois. She looks so sweet lying there in the casket."

But Granny Hunt insisted that her maid take the soup. A few seconds later Granny heard the maid scream, then the bowl crashed to the floor. She ran into the parlor to see what had happened.

Granny saw her maid pointing a very shaky finger at the casket.

With her eyes wide open and her mouth gaping, "She moved!"

Granny's eyes followed the direction of Immediately the nurse administered artificial re Lois was still unconscious, she was soon breathing normally with a good strong heartbeat.

The doctor soon arrived, shaken and disbelieving. He claimed he had performed all the necessary steps before pronouncing her dead. He insisted he had not detected a heartbeat or breathing. He had even placed a mirror before her face and it had shown no moisture on the surface. This was indeed a miracle.

After Lois's recovery, Granny told her the story and told her about the deaths of her mother and older sister. She even took Lois to show her the little casket in which she had once been placed. Mama remembers it being a little white casket and how pretty she thought it was inside.

My mother is now quite old. She has made us all promise that when she dies "again" we will have her cremated.

7

The Old Schoolhouse

Micanopy

My first book of ghost stories had been out for only a short time. I would say about two months. One day I was delivering a second order of books to the shop Southern Expressions in Micanopy, Florida. Laurel, the assistant manager, and I were talking about how well my book was doing and she asked if I had heard about the ghost in the old schoolhouse.

I told her, "No, but I would love to hear about it because my mother taught there around nineteen-twenty-five and my grandmother taught there until her death in nineteen-thirteen."

The store was not very busy at the time, so Laurel told me what she knew about the ghost. Laurel is a very young lady in her early twenties, so her story was very recent.

She said, "All I know for sure is this: when any students or I went there, we always had our meetings on the second floor. No one would go upstairs alone because of the things that happened."

"What sort of things?" I asked.

"Well, we would hear strange noises and other sounds that were very scary to us."

"What kind of sounds were they?" I asked.

"Well, I heard squeaking sounds, like someone coming up the

stairs, but there were no stairs where the sounds seemed to be coming from. It was just a weird feeling that I had about the place, and I personally didn't want to be alone."

I thanked her and told her I would check into the story further to see what else I could find out about the old school.

I spoke to another lady who lived in Micanopy for years. She told me she had not personally seen or heard anything there, but she had heard that the second floor was haunted. She had also been told that it was haunted by one of the school teachers and her family, who had some kind of disease and died around the turn of the century. She is supposed to be looking for some of her children.

This really intrigued me because it was very close to what had really happened to my grandmother's family. My grandmother was teaching school there in 1913 when my mother came down with typhoid fever. The doctor didn't expect her to live (see "Living Miracle," in chapter six, for the full story). After my mother went into a coma, her mother and older sister came down with typhoid and died within a week of each other. Friends took in mother's younger sister, Julia, so she wouldn't catch it.

A week or so later my wife and I went over to Lake City, Florida, to visit my mother, who was ninety-five years old and living in a nursing home there. We asked her if she had ever heard of any ghost at the old school.

She looked a little startled, and then replied. "Yes. After being out for about a year, I went back to the school and I remember that none of us wanted to go upstairs alone because of the noises we heard. They seemed to always come from the top of the stairs in the middle of the building. We heard crying or soft sobbing. We couldn't hold our meeting up there either without the whole group."

"Then you actually heard the sound yourself?" I asked.

"Sure I did, many times, along with the other girls. But for some reason I never did get as afraid as the others."

Then I told her what I had heard in Micanopy. She was amazed at the closeness of the story I had heard and our family history.

She turned to me and asked, "Robert, do think it could have been Mama and Esther looking for me and Julia? She would not have known that I didn't die, or what became of Julia. She was sent to Mrs. Knots so she wouldn't get sick."

Before we left I asked Mama to describe to me where Esther's and her mother's classroom was.

"We would come in the front door, and the stairs were directly in front of us. We would go up the stairs and turn left. Mama's room was the first room on the right. Or if you stood in front of the schoolhouse, her room was on the second floor, left corner. Esther was in Mama's class."

The next week my wife and I drove over to Micanopy and went

to the old school. The students now are all bused to Gainesville and the Old Schoolhouse is now the town hall and library.

As we went through the front doors we saw something a little different from the description my mother had given to me. There were no stairs in the middle of the hall as she had described; they were over on the left as we entered. We walked further down the hall and told the lady in the office that my mother and grandmother had taught school there and we were wondering if it would be all right if we looked around a bit. She said that it would be fine, take our time.

Then I turned back to her and asked her about the stairs. My mother had described them as being in the middle of the hall. The lady smiled and said, "Originally, they were in the middle of the hall, but they were moved to the side years ago. I can't remember just when they were changed, but there are pictures of them in that location."

My wife and I went up the stairs to look around. The rooms up there were now used as meeting rooms. As we turned and started down, I heard an indescribable noise and had a warm feeling. It seemed as if someone had just taken a deep breath—a kind of wheezing sound. It came from the direction of my grandmother's old classroom. I turned to my wife at the same time she turned to me. "Did you hear that," we said together.

Now I know why some had heard sounds coming from the middle of the upstairs hall. That was where the stairs used to be.

I don't know if somehow this ghost is my grandmother but the facts are that my mother took sick with typhoid fever at about the end of the school year in 1913. Shortly after that her mother and her sister Esther took sick and died within a week.

Could my grandmother have somehow known who I was when I went up those stairs? I may never know for sure or maybe not until I go to meet them face-to-face. In the meantime though, no one has told me anything bad about these ghosts. So if you should encounter them someday, just say hello and go on your way. I'm sure there will be no problems.

8
The Big Scare
Archer

Many years ago, my father's family told a story of my father's brother, George, when he was a young boy. They lived in the small town of Archer in north central Florida.

As the story went, George was a very studious young man and worked in the local drugstore—the only drugstore in town—because he wanted so badly to become a pharmacist someday. The family didn't have much money, so he knew that the only hope for him to do this was to get a scholarship to college.

It seems that George was very much afraid of the dark and, if at all possible, would not go out alone at night. That was probably because my dad, William, who was the oldest, believed in ghosts and was always telling ghost stories.

One day, when it came time for George to get off work, no one came to get him. The later it got, the more concerned he became, not wanting to admit that he was afraid of the dark. Finally, the druggist asked him if anything was the matter. George said no, that he was just waiting for his sister and she may need something from the store. He didn't want to say that he was afraid of walking home alone in the dark. The druggist said all right, but he would be locking up soon. George said he would wait until then just to see if she came.

Now, by city standards, he only had to walk a few blocks. Home was just on the other side of a big field, which he could cut across by taking a path. In the country this seemed much farther because there were no city lights. And that night there was only a partial moon. This made it very dark. The field had grown up with lots of trees and bushes. George hated that place even when someone came for him. He was always seeing things hiding in the dark.

William had told George that many people had disappeared in that field, never to be seen or heard from again. He had even told George story about the Indian, Old Wildcat, who haunted the woods. Of course, these were the things George remembered the most.

Anyway, after a while the druggist told him, "George, I'm going to close up now. It doesn't look like anyone is going to come, so you had better head on home."

Very slowly and reluctantly, George started off down the dirt road. When he came to the path through the field he stopped, hoping someone would show up for him, but he didn't see or hear anyone coming. After waiting a few minutes, he started off down the path, not wanting to walk the long way home around the field.

George had walked about fifty feet into the empty lot when he heard a hoot owl cry, "WHOO! WHOOOO!"

When the owl did that, George jumped off the path, stepped on a tree limb, and fell on his face in the bushes. He picked himself up and started off again very slowly, not wanting to disturb anything that might be in bushes. George had walked about five or six feet when he felt something pull on his jacket. He turned around to see what it was, hoping one of the girls or William had come for him, but no one was there. The clouds had cleared up some and he could see pretty well, but there just wasn't anyone or anything there at all, so he started off again down the path. Every time he would take a few steps, something would pull at his jacket. He was really getting scared now. He could see that nothing and no one was there. He tried to walk faster, but when he did, it pulled harder at his jacket. The sweat was beginning to pour down the sides of his face. His eyes were getting bigger and bigger with each step and tug at his jacket. He even thought to himself, "If I ever get home, I'll never go through this field again."

Now he was taking slow steps. There wasn't the quick pull on his jacket like before. It was more like a steady pressure, as though someone or something wanted him to stay.

Just about that time, the old owl let out another "WHOOO! WHOOOO!"

And that was it. George took off like a bullet. Whatever it was would have to catch him now. He wasn't going to be taken easily. He took off his coat as he ran. If it wanted that coat, it could have it. He was home in a flash. He hit the front porch from the ground in two steps and burst into the house. The family was all sitting around the room and asked, "George, what in the world is wrong?"

Between gasps for breath, he tried to tell them how the ghost had tried to take him by pulling on his jacket and how it wouldn't let him go. He just knew he would never see any of them ever again.

William listened to the story for a little while and then said he would go back down the path and get George's jacket. William wasn't gone long when they heard him on the porch laughing softly. As he came in, he was holding George's jacket and laughing. They all asked, "What's so funny, William?"

William walked over to George. "Were you bringing something home for Mama?" he asked.

George said, "Yes! A spool of thread. It's in my jacket pocket. Why?"

Holding up the spool, William asked, "Is this it?"

"Yes," George said, "but that one is empty. There is no thread on it."

William replied, "Yes, it is the spool, but the thread is all the way back down the path. I'm afraid that's your ghost."

In unison, George and his sister asked, "How?"

William continued, "Well, when you fell at the start of the path, the thread caught on a bush, but the spool was still in your pocket. Every time you took a step, the thread would pull the spool, making you think something had you by the coattail. The faster you walked or ran, the harder it pulled, until you ran out of thread."

They all had a big laugh, and after George finished blushing, he laughed, too. He told William that something would scare him, too, someday. But that's another story.

Uncle George did go on to get his Ph.D. in pharmacy. He taught for a few years, then decided to become a medical doctor. He has practiced medicine for many years.

George, I am told, would never again go down that path alone at night. He would stay at the store until someone came, even if it was way after the store had closed.

9

The Indian

Archer

This is a ghost story my father told me many years ago. He swore that every word is true and that he would go to his grave knowing it to be so. My father told it again to my wife and me the last time we saw him in the hospital just before he died.

The story takes place when my dad was just a young boy in Archer, Florida, around 1917. My father had been to a friend's house and was walking home late one afternoon through a section of woods that was a shortcut from town to the house. As he was walking down the path admiring the woods and birds, he happened to look up the path about thirty yards. There in the middle of the path was an Indian dressed in a cloth, with his face painted and wearing a turban. The Indian had a bow with an arrow drawn and was aiming it right at my dad. As the Indian let his arrow fly, Dad jumped behind the nearest tree. He claimed that he heard the arrow hit the tree he was hiding behind. Dad waited, listening for the Indian to come up to him. Not hearing anything after a couple of minutes, he came out from behind the tree for a better view. The Indian was nowhere in sight. He looked up at the tree where the arrow had hit. There was no arrow in the tree, nor was there a mark where it had hit the tree. Dad then walked up the path to where he had first seen the Indian. It was a dirt path, but there were no footprints or marks on the ground to show that anyone had been there. He looked a good ten feet on either side of where he knew the Indian had been, but all he saw were his own footprints in the dirt. He went home very cautiously, watching for the Indian, but he saw no other signs.

When he got home, he didn't tell anyone what had happened because he didn't want anyone to laugh at him or think he was crazy. After having supper with the rest of the family, he went out on the porch and was sitting on the steps when his father came out and said, "William, you were mighty quiet tonight. Is there anything the matter?"

Dad said, "No. I was just thinking. It wasn't anything important." After a little bit, he said, "Pa, some of the boys in town were saying that there were some Indians in these parts. Are there any?"

"No, son, I don't remember hearing of any round here for over forty years. The last one I remember hearing about was Old Wildcat—that's what we called him, but I don't know if that was his real name. He was hanged right over there in those woods between here and town. I was just a boy about your age, but I remember it as though it happened just yesterday. The story goes that a man and wife had been killed by some renegade Indians over on the other side of town. When the posse went out looking for them, all they found was Old Wildcat camped in the woods over there. The men in the posse grabbed him up, with him saying all the time that he didn't do it. He kept telling them that he didn't know anything about it, but they were tired, dirty, and angry. They got a rope and strung him up to an old oak tree about halfway down the path. Before the wagon was pulled out from under him, he swore he would come back because he didn't do this thing. I'll never forget that look in his eyes before he fell. It was a look of pure hate. I could almost see the fire in them."

Dad asked his Pa, "Did he do it?"

"I don't know for sure, son, but I don't think that he did." His Pa told him that over the years, many of the young people claimed to have seen Old Wildcat in those woods with his bow and arrows. Some of the old people even claim he comes back to make the families of the men who killed him pay. The story is that two of the men that led the hanging party were found dead down the path. They had a look of fear and horror on their faces. Not a mark was ever found on any of them.

Dad asked his Pa, "Have you ever seen Old Wildcat?"

"Yes, son, I have—many years ago, when I was a boy, before we moved from here to Palatka. I was coming home from town and there in the middle of the path was Old Wildcat, dressed just as he was the day they hanged him, except for the war paint. He had his bow and arrow pointed at me."

Dad said, "What did you do? What did you do then, Pa?"

His father looked real hard at my Dad a few seconds, then said, "I stood there and got killed!" Then his Dad started to laugh.

It was about a week before my Dad had a reason to go down that path again. He had almost forgotten the incident, or at least put it in the back of his mind like he had only dreamed it. Old Wildcat was far from his mind as he walked down the path. Then, all of a sudden, he felt a cold wind blow past him. When he looked up the path, there was Old Wildcat standing right in front of him about twenty-five feet away. He could see the fire in his eyes that his Pa had told him about. Again, he had the bow pulled. Without thinking, Dad jumped behind the nearest tree again. Looking back, he saw the Indian standing there with his hands down his sides, a look of sadness on his face as he faded away. Dad came out from behind the tree, looked up to where he had heard the arrow hit, knowing that it wouldn't be there. He walked home and into his room, not saying a word to anyone.

Later that night after supper, his mother came over to him and asked, "What's the matter, William? Are you and Muriel having problems?"

"No, Mama, I'm just thinking."

He was sitting there on the porch swing when his Pa said, "William, have you seen Old Wildcat again?"

"Yes, Pa, on the way home again today." Then he told him everything that had happened both times.

Pa said, "William, there is only one thing you can do! You've got to stand up to him."

"But how, Pa? He's a ghost!

"I know, but you must not show fear. You can handle it."

Dad stayed awake all night thinking about what he had to do. The next day, he went out and sat under the old oak tree where they had hanged Wildcat and waited. The sun was just about down when he felt that cold wind pass by.

Without even looking up, he spoke. "Wildcat, I know you're there and I want you to know that I'm not afraid of you. I have never done you any harm and I don't know anyone who has. I have a right to be here in these woods, and a right to walk this path, and I'm going to. So do what you will."

Dad looked up just as Old Wildcat was fading away, but this time he said that he could almost see a smile on the old Indian's face just before he vanished.

When Dad got home for supper, everyone knew he was much better, but no one except his feather knew what had really happened. That night on the porch, all his Pa said was, "You did it, didn't you?"

Dad said, "Yes, sir, I did."

Then his Pa said, "He won't bother you again, son."

Sure enough, my Dad walked that path hundreds of times after that, both night and day, but he never saw the old Indian again. A few years after that, he was sitting in the woods out under the same old oak tree. He saw what appeared to be two small bumps in the tree, about where those arrows had hit it. He used his pocketknife to pull the bark away, and out fell two arrowheads. Dad kept those arrowheads, and no one could ever tell him that there was no such thing as ghosts, but he wasn't afraid of them ever again.

10

The Lady in White

Starke

The present owner of the house told this story to me. His story begins a few years ago when he bought the old house on Cherry Street. At the time, he didn't know how old the house was, but was told it was at least one hundred years old. Even though it was run-down and had not been lived in for a number of years, he could tell it had been very beautiful and majestic in its day. He told me that many people indicated to him that the house was used during World War II as a hotel for the family members of the soldiers, because of so many soldiers at Camp Blanding. Starke had always been a small town, but loved by those who lived there. The big old house had two stories, with porches all the way around both floors. Before the new owner started to remodel it, vagrants had been known to set up housekeeping for a time. While he was working on it, he lived in a small portion of the house and sometimes allowed the police to use the other part to train officers in searching for drugs. Here is his story of the haunting.

I have always been the type of person who doesn't believe in ghosts or spirits, so it really didn't bother me when some people in Starke told me the house was haunted. I would smile and listen politely, then go on about my business, not really paying much attention to their stories.

One night, shortly after I started working on and living in the

house, the first in a series of events took place. The night was warm and clear with a light breeze. It was quite comfortable in the house because of its high ceilings. That night I was really tired after a hard day at work. Before getting ready for bed I took out my wallet, keys, and change from my pockets, laid them on the dresser, and then climbed into bed.

Early the next morning, as I was getting dressed, I went to the dresser and put my wallet in my pocket. But my keys were not where I had put them. After a brief search, I found them across the room on the night stand. That was very strange; I must have been more tired than I had thought. But I didn't think much of it.

Then a few days later it happened again—and then again. I was positive, then, that wherever I put them at night, they would be moved. I decided to sit up in a chair one night, to see what was happening. Sometime well past midnight, I was startled to hear what sounded like someone getting up out of the water bed. I immediately turned on the lights and looked at the bed. It was moving, just as if someone had just gotten up off of it. I instinctively looked over at the dresser where I had put my keys just a few hours before. They were gone. Again I found them on the night stand across the room. I knew then that something very strange was happening.

On another occasion someone knocking on my door awakened me. I answered the door to find a policeman standing there; he told me he was driving by and saw a young woman standing on the porch in the section of the house I had not started to work on yet.

I put on my robe and went with him to that part of the house. We looked all around. He told me she was wearing a long white dress, much like those worn at the turn of the century. She appeared to be in her early twenties and very pretty.

I told the officer I had no idea who it could be, but I thanked him for stopping. He told me he would keep an eye on the place just in case it was vagrants or drug users. Old houses like this are sometimes used that way if they think no one lives there.

I thanked him again and he left.

Others have reported seeing this young woman in white at the windows, in the halls, and out on the porches upstairs.

Another incident took place the day some of the police were placing contraband around the rooms for the others to find later. The officer reported he could feel someone watching him. As he turned, he saw a young girl dressed in white standing in the doorway. She was just standing there watching him, but not saying anything.

"Hi," he said as he got up off the floor, "may I help you with something?" When he looked again, the young woman was gone. Running to the door and looking down the halls, he saw nothing. She was gone!

Many people have reported seeing my Lady in White. Some have even said they had tried to talk with her, without success. We have all wondered who she may be or may have been. No one seems to know for sure.

Some say a young girl stayed in the house in 1918, and died there when she found out the man she loved had been killed in France during World War I. This is the story I like best.

But whoever she is or was, there is no record of her harming or trying to harm anyone. Why she moved the keys no one knows, except that maybe she just didn't want them where I had put them.

Some say when she is near, they feel a cool breeze and smell a slight hint of lavender perfume.

I can't say what would happen to anyone who came into this old house if he or she was up to no good. Our Lady in White just may see that he or she leaves a bit quicker than intended.

11

The Specters
at Ocean Pond

Olustee State Park

A very good friend told me this story many years ago. I had no reason to doubt or believe anything he told me, but at the time, I did not believe in ghosts, spirits, or that sort of thing. Being the good friends we were, there was no way I would tell him that. To protect his privacy, I will call him James in this story. This is the way he told it to me.

Some friends and I had gone water skiing on Ocean Pond and had decided to spend the night in the campground. Olustee State Park is located on U.S. 90 between Baldwin and Lake City, Florida. After we finished cooking hot dogs on the campfire, we were just sitting around the fire telling stories or, as we would say, swapping lies. That's when we heard it. *Bang! Bang! Pop! Pop!* Then what sounded like horses and men running through the palmettos.

"What in the world was that?" Bill asked.

"I don't know," replied James, "but let's go find out."

"There sure seems to be something big going on," Roger said.

We took off down the path through the trees toward the sounds of the commotion. It was just beginning to get dark and the ground fog had begun coming in off the lake. As we broke through the trees and could see the lake through the fog, we stopped in our tracks. Our eyes were wide open in amazement. We looked at each other and said as one, "Are we dreaming?"

James said, "If we are, we're all having the same dream."

There before us was a battle, a Civil War battle. Men were running into the pond and were being killed by men in gray. Most of the other soldiers seemed to be black. It was a real massacre.

We could see the fog thickening out on the lake and coming toward the shore and the soldiers. As the fog came ashore and covered the fighting men, all sound stopped, no more guns firing, no more screaming men—nothing! Not a sound! The quiet seemed eerie.

We waited for quite some time, then walked over to the lake where we had seen the battle. Nothing was there—not one sign of any type of battle. We couldn't even find their footprints. It was a sure thing that none of us would get any sleep that night! We spent most of the night talking about what we had just heard and seen.

Had we encountered the spirits of men who had fought in the Battle of Olustee? Over the years we told the story to a few friends, but I'm not sure whether they were just being polite or whether they believed us. For what it's worth, none of us even had a beer.

As I told you, I didn't truly believe my friend's story myself until much later, even though I never forgot James telling it.

My own story began in the late 1960s. I had gone camping with my family. After we finished supper and got the kids to bed, we heard gunshots over by the lake and we could hear men screaming.

"What is that?" my wife said.

"I don't know," I told her, "but I'll go find out."

"Now you be careful," my wife said as I went off toward the lake.

I hadn't gone far when the fog became so thick that I could hardly see. Then I heard crying over to my right. As I came to an oak tree, there huddled on the ground was a very frightened black man, dressed in a Union Army uniform. When our eyes met, all he could say was, "Please, massa, don't let them kill me, we was only doing what we was made to do."

I told him I had no intention of hurting him. I asked if he was hurt, and he told me no, but he knew the soldiers would kill him if they found him. "They tries to kill all us black Union soldiers."

"You don't have to worry" I told him, "I won't give you away." I then turned away and listened to the quiet of the night. But the most amazing thing was, when I turned back to him, he was gone.

I looked all around the area, but there was no sign of him. He had just vanished. The silence startled me too. No longer could I hear any of the other soldiers down by the pond.

Over the years I have heard others tell of strange apparitions they have encountered in and around the old Olustee battlefield. The men in the area do re-enactments of the Battle of Olustee every year now, and thousands come from all over to watch because it is so well done.

With all of the sights, sounds, and other out-of-the-ordinary phenomena, no one has ever reported having a truly bad feeling when they sighted one or more of the ghosts of the Battle of Olustee.

I have studied the history of the Battle of Olustee, also known as the Battle of Ocean Pond and the Battle to Save Florida, and found that it was the only big battle fought in Florida during the Civil War and it ended in a resounding defeat of the Union Army.

Come over and visit the park; the rangers may have something new to tell you. And you can enjoy learning the history of the greatest battle fought in Florida during the Civil War.

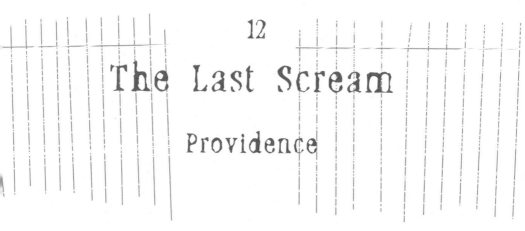

12

The Last Scream

Providence

This was not the first time anyone had heard screams in the old city cemetery, but no one had really ever seen anything. The weather was a little cool that night many years ago when Jesse and Will reported the screams and moaning coming from down there. I remember now how frightened they had been. Over the years they had upset many people with their pranks as someone would pass the cemetery, but that night it was their turn.

It was the middle of October 1920 when the story began. No one had even started to think about Halloween, much less begun planning any tricks or pranks to play on anyone.

Walker Dawson—or Uncle Walker, as he was affectionately known—had gone to town in Worthington Springs that night to talk with his friends when Will and Jesse burst in through the front door. They were out of breath from running all the way from the cemetery. After they calmed down a bit, they told their story.

"Boys, I know you're having your fun, but I wish you would not have it at the expense of my Winnie. She was only fifteen and I miss her very much, so if you must play your pranks, do so on someone else. I would appreciate it," Uncle Walker said.

Will and Jesse were a little startled, then spoke in unison. "Mr.

Dawson, we're sorry and don't mean any disrespect, but we ain't playing no joke. We did hear those screams and moans just like we told it."

Uncle Walker was getting a little upset now and said, "All right, boys, I've heard enough. You come with me."

"Where to, sir?"

"You're going to take me to where you heard that scream, and if you're lying, your folks will hear about it. You know what that will mean."

Swearing they were not lying, they all left for the cemetery. The boys showed Uncle Walker where they were when they first heard the scream.

"We was walking down this path talking when we heard the first scream coming from over there," Will said, pointing toward Winnie's grave. "At first we thought someone was playing a trick on us because last year we had played one on Winnie at about this same spot. Jesse and me called out that we knowed who was there, trying to get them to come out. Then we heard another scream. It sounded kind of funny. Like it was close, yet far off. You know what I mean."

Jesse spoke up then, "We went all around the area listening for anything unusual or any sounds that may have been out of the ordinary, but we didn't hear anything else, except those way off moans and then crying."

Uncle Walker felt that the boys were telling the truth as they believed it to be. Either someone had been playing a trick on them or their guilt had taken over and made them think they had heard something. Either way, he told them to go home, but to think about it in the future and find some other way to have their fun.

Nothing else was ever said about it. As far as we knew, Jesse and Will never played pranks in the cemetery again. In fact, they wouldn't even go through it at night and would seldom walk through it during the day.

Then one day about a year later, a man from the county came by Uncle Walker's house and told him the county was going to put a road through the cemetery and some of the graves would have to be moved. His daughter's grave was one of them. The man told him that the county would pay all of the expenses and do all the moving. They just wanted to tell him what was happening and that if he wanted to come down and see that everything was done with respect, he was more than welcome to do so.

Uncle Walker thanked the man and told him that he would come down there to see the new site for the grave.

On the day of the move, Uncle Walker and some of his sons were there, just as he said they would be. They watched as the grave was opened and the casket was laid on the pile of dirt until the truck could come and take it to the new site. They stood there looking at it for a

en, turning to his sons, Uncle Walker said, "Boys, I've
at casket."

ried to talk him out of it, saying it had been a long time
and he really didn't want to see Winnie that way. He would not be
swayed and they all watched as he approached the casket and slowly
lifted the lid. No sooner was the lid lifted when Uncle Walker fell to
his knees clutching his chest and saying, "Oh, Lord God, no!" Then
he started to sob.

His boys ran to him. "Dad, what's wrong?"

Their eyes fell on the casket at the same time. You could see the look
of absolute horror on their faces as they stood motionless beside it.

The workmen moved over and looked inside. They turned away
with looks of shock and horror. There inside the casket lay the remains
of Winnie, but she was on her stomach with both hands in her hair.
Her head was turned to the right, her mouth open as though she had
been cut off in mid-scream. Her last scream.

Everyone knew then what Will and Jesse had heard in the cemetery that night a year ago. Winnie had been buried alive. When she
awoke, she only had air enough for those last screams after realizing
where she was.

To this day, it is still told that people sometimes hear strange
sounds at night coming from the old cemetery near Providence. Go
by some night—you may see or hear something too.

13

Ashlyn

Lake City

For Lake City, Florida, it was a cold and windy night in February. Roger had been out cutting wood for the fireplace in the big old house he and his wife had recently bought. He brought the wood in and placed it in the wood box and started a fire. His wife had gone to visit her sister and wouldn't be home for at least a week. But Roger didn't mind, he had been waiting to catch up on his reading anyway.

After Roger had taken his shower, he pulled his big lounge chair closer to the fire and started reading his new book. He had read for an hour or so, and stopped to put another log on the fire. As he did, he felt a cold chill on his neck as though someone were watching him. Roger turned around, but no one was there. He checked all the windows and doors to be sure everything was locked and secure before he continued his reading. He read until he got tired, then decided to turn in for the night.

Roger didn't know how long he had been asleep when he heard what sounded like someone humming and rocking back and forth downstairs. He eased out of bed, put on his robe, and started downstairs. When he got about halfway down he could see someone rocking in his chair in front of the fireplace. Slowly he descended the rest of the way. He could then see that it was a young lady about thirty

years of age. She was knitting and humming as she rocked back and forth. Roger spoke to her.

"Well, hello. I don't believe we've met, have we?"

The girl jumped up, a little startled, and turned to face him. Roger saw that she was very beautiful; her long black hair fell down below her waist. Her big, almond-shaped, blue-green eyes held a startled expression as he spoke. Her complexion was very light. She wore a lace housecoat over her nightgown. Her breathtaking beauty held him speechless for a few moments. Then Roger spoke again.

"How did you get in here? I know this is a very stupid thing for me to say, but I do live here."

She said, "Roger, I'm Ashlyn. Don't you know me?"

Roger turned to look behind him and started to say something, then he turned back to her. She was gone! He sat down and shook his head, attempting to clear his thinking. Was he crazy or sleepwalking, he thought to himself. She had seemed so real. He even thought he could smell her sweet, light perfume still lingering in the room. Roger looked all over the house before going to bed.

He didn't sleep much that night, to be sure. He couldn't get that name—Ashlyn—out of his head. Why did it seem so familiar? He didn't know anyone by that name. Finally he decided that it must have been a dream, because he surely didn't believe in ghosts.

For days Roger couldn't get Ashlyn out of his mind. She seemed so familiar yet he knew they hadn't met. How did he know her and how did she know his name? He kept going over and over these questions in his mind.

Then one night while Roger was up late again reading in the living room alone, he thought he could smell the light, sweet fragrance of Ashlyn's perfume. He looked up from his book and there she was standing by the fireplace. She looked at him but didn't say anything.

"Well, how are you, Ashlyn?" Roger said. "I haven't seen you in a while and I was afraid I had said something to upset you. If I did, I'm sorry, it was not intended. Come over by my chair and let's talk a bit, okay?"

She hesitated for a moment. Then without saying a word, she came over and sat on the hearth in front of the fireplace.

"You really have the advantage over me, Miss Ashlyn. You seem to know me, but I don't know you. Why do you think that is?"

Roger waited for her reply for what seemed an eternity. Then very softly she spoke. "I must give you time to remember."

"Can't you at least give me a hint as to when and where we knew each other?"

"It was many, many years ago, here in this house. But you must remember on your own."

"Was it by chance in another life?"

"You will remember Roger. Just keep trying."

From the top of the stairs Roger's wife called, "Roger, do we have company or are you talking to yourself?"

"Oh, it's nothing dear, just the television."

"Well, turn it down. I have to get up early tomorrow."

"All right dear, I'll be up soon. Good night." He turned back to where Ashlyn had been sitting. She was gone.

For the next few days Roger checked with many of the local people about the history of the old house he had bought. Did anyone know anything about a young lady by the name of Ashlyn?

Then he stopped by the Historical Museum and asked them. One lady who had lived in Lake City all her life remembered something. When she was a small child, her family told her and her sister that the old house was haunted. They stayed away, but she was told that a great many people claimed to pass by the old house at night and see light coming from the living room. Some even said they crept up to the window and saw a beautiful black-haired lady standing by the fireplace crying. But she had never seen her. She also heard that the woman haunts the house waiting for her true love to return.

Roger asked if she knew anywhere he might find more information.

She told him to check with the local newspaper obituaries around the turn of the century. He read for at least a couple of hours without any success. Then as he was just about to give up, he saw it. There, on one of the back pages, was a picture of the girl in the house. Roger read the caption under the picture. "Local girl found dead by her fiancé in her living room. No foul play suspected." He had a copy of the article made to take home and study more closely.

That evening after his wife had gone to bed, Roger read the article. It said, "Local girl found dead in her home here in Lake ⟨

Ashlyn Geer was found lying by the fireplace in the living room. Roger, her fiancé, had just returned from Havana, Cuba, after serving in the Rough Riders with Colonel Roosevelt and was in hopes of surprising her. Upon further investigation by this reporter, it was discovered that Miss Geer had received word a few days earlier that Roger Mills had been killed in a charge up San Juan Hill with his regiment. Miss Geer's friends say she was completely heartbroken over Roger's death, and no one had seen her for about three days."

The Medical Examiner reported no signs of foul play and that she had been dead about two days before the body was found. Roger had been in south Florida, waiting for the train to bring him to Lake City. The only cause of death reported was that she had died of a broken heart.

The article said that Roger stayed for the funeral services, then told their friends he would go west. He couldn't stand the pain of losing his beloved Ashlyn.

Roger looked at the photo again and knew this was his Ashlyn. As he stared at the picture, he felt a presence in the room. Looking up, Ashlyn was standing in front of him.

"I see you know," she said.

"Yes, I know, but can this be true?"

"I have been waiting for you, Roger," she said, "I knew that someday you would return to me."

Roger reached for her and could feel her presence close to him.

For months after that, Roger's friends could see a difference in him. His wife said that he had told her about Ashlyn, but she thought he was going over the edge. Roger would stay up, many times all night, talking to someone in the living room that she never saw. His wife finally decided to force Roger to get medical help.

A short time after that, she found Roger sitting in his chair holding the clipping from the newspaper with Ashlyn's picture. He must have had a heart attack and died sometime during the night.

A few weeks after the funeral Roger's wife was going through the closet, when she felt something way back on one of the top shelves. She got a chair and took it down. It was a picture frame; as she turned it over, she let out a gasp. For there in her hands, she was holding a photograph of a beautiful, young, dark-haired girl with a soldier getting ready to board a ship in Jacksonville, Florida. There was no doubt that the girl was Ashlyn. The strangest thing of all was that there also was no doubt that the young soldier was Roger, her Roger.

No one has ever reported seeing Ashlyn or Roger again. I would like to think that they are together and happy at last.

14

Phantom on the Beach

Jacksonville

The summer of 1949 was very hot. Bill had just made the Lifeguard Corps at Jacksonville Beach. He had worked hard that winter completing the Red Cross Senior Life Saving Course and First Aid. The new recruits had also finished their two weeks of beach training, which was required before one was allowed to man a tower alone. It had been very hard work, and his chest was a little bigger with pride in wearing the beach's lifeguard swimsuit and carrying his torpedo buoy with him. He could remember how he used to look up to the beach guards in awe. Knowing how the mothers would put their little ones in the water close to the towers, they also had a tradition to live up to. The Corps for Jacksonville Beach had not lost a swimmer under their protection for over three years.

Bill's first day alone in the tower went very well. The worst things that happened were a few jellyfish stings. For his first weekend, the weather was great and the forecast was for it to stay that way. Everyone expected a huge crowd, so they were all told to be on their toes at all times, especially in front of the boardwalk areas directly in front of them. As a new guard, Bill was placed in tower number 17, way down the beach. They would rotate every two hours. When the truck got to Bill's station, everyone else had been placed. Bill jumped off the truck with his flag, buoy, and first aid kit.

There wasn't anyone swimming in Bill's area yet, so he had plenty of time to set up. He pulled his tower down to the high water mark, put his flag in the holder behind his seat and the first aid kit on its rack, and climbed into his seat looking out over the water. He watched the birds and pelicans diving for fish and the little sandpipers running along the sand as the tide came in and rolled out. Now and then, out in the water beyond the breakers, he saw a pod of porpoises play and roll.

After about thirty or forty minutes, it was time to move his tower back with the tide. Bill stood up and started to climb down when he thought he saw someone swimming just a little beyond the outside breakers. He strained to look closer, but saw nothing. Thinking he had been mistaken, he continued to move.

Bill had been on his post for about an hour and a half when he saw it again. This time it looked like a young girl swimming. The movements were so swift and smooth, though, that he thought it must have been another dolphin—but he could have sworn it had long brown hair. People were beginning to come now, so he couldn't look much. He had to watch them.

Just before Bill was relieved, he saw her again. She rose out of the water about waist high and waved to him. Bill waved back, knowing that she must be standing on a sandbar. From this distance, he couldn't see how old she was. He could only see that she was beautiful with that long brown hair. He didn't see any more of her that day. All week, he only saw her while assigned to tower 17.

The following Saturday, Bill was assigned to tower 17 again; he was told that he would probably have to stay there all day because of the double-up on the boardwalk crews. A nor'easter was up so the waves were about three feet tall. People began coming to the beach early. One lady came with her little daughter and put a blanket down right next to his tower. The little girl was a cute, blonde-haired, blue-eyed child, about three or four years old.

He overheard her mother tell her to stay right there in front of the lifeguard while she went back to the car for suntan lotion, then her mother left. Bill never could understand parents like that. The little girl's name was Cathy. Bill saw her play in the sand for a bit, then start to wander closer to the water. Cathy sat down in about four inches of water, which was no problem, and Bill continued his surveillance of the beach. When he looked down again to where Cathy should be, she was gone! He looked every direction, up and down the beach, but no Cathy. Then, out beyond the first breakers, Bill saw something yellow on the surface. He threw his flag down, grabbed his buoy and headed for the spot where he had seen something. He dove down once and saw nothing, came up for air, then went down again. Then he saw the brown-haired swimmer coming toward him. She had Cathy in her arms. She pushed her to Bill as he popped out of the water. He swam to shore with little Cathy, who was unconscious. He laid her on the blanket on her stomach to pump out the water and resuscitate her. Just as she was coming around, the lifeguard truck drove up. Her mother came up at the same time, almost hysterical, and Cathy started to cry. The patrol captain told the mother that they should take Cathy to the station for the nurse to look after her, and when she agreed, off they went. Bill turned to find the brown-haired swimmer to thank her, but she was gone.

A couple of hours later, the truck came back with Cathy and her mother. Her mother thanked him again and again. Little Cathy looked up at Bill again and said, "Mr. Lifeguard, where's the girl fish?"

He said, "I don't know, Cathy. I wish I did."

The captain patted Bill on the shoulder and said, "Good work,

Bill. Staying alert saved a life today. See you at the station in about an hour."

Monday was his day off and Bill decided to go down to tower 17 to see if he could find his brown-haired helper. He took a little sail canoe with an outrigger and was just outside the breakers when he put out his sea anchor. He hadn't been there long when something took hold of the outrigger. He looked over, and there was the brown-haired girl, holding on to the side.

"Hi!" Bill said, "Come aboard. I've been looking for you."

She pulled up a little higher on the side, but didn't come in the boat. Bill could see that she was much prettier up close. She was about his age. Her brown hair flowed to below her waist and it even had sea-weeds in it. Her eyes were a light brown and her skin was very light, almost pale, which seemed very unusual to Bill since she stayed in the water so much. He said, "I tried to find you to thank you yesterday, but when I looked around for you, you were gone. Do you live near here?"

Very softly she said, "Yes."

He asked her name.

She smiled at him, her eyes sparkling, and told him, "Lonnie." Then she said, "I have to go now."

Bill asked when he could see her again, and she told him that she took a walk on the beach every night after nine o'clock, then she dove under the water and was gone. Bill thought she had the best lungs in the world to be able to stay under so long. He thought he would ask her to teach him how to do that.

That night, Bill had his dinner at the station, cleaned up, and headed to number 17 tower. He got there about five after nine, but no one was there, so he decided to sit on the rocks and wait. It hadn't been more than ten minutes when he felt a cold breeze blow past and something touched his arm. As he turned, there she stood. He was a little startled at first because he hadn't seen or heard her coming down the beach. It was like a phantom in the night. He asked her how she did that. She just shrugged her shoulders and smiled. Lonnie was dressed in sandals, dark shorts, and a Hawaiian shirt. He took her hand and said, "Ready to take that walk now?"

They walked for about an hour down the beach in one direction, then turned and started back. He never let go of her hand, nor she his. When they got back to the rocks, Lonnie said that she had to go. Bill asked her when he would see her again. All she said was, "I'll be around when you want me."

She seemed to float over to him and he kissed her. He said that she tasted as fresh as the ocean itself. He turned to pick up his shoes and when he looked back, she was gone. This puzzled him because he could see quite a way down the beach in both directions and saw nothing.

The next day was the beginning of Memorial Day weekend, one of the busiest weekends of the season because it marked the beginning of summer. The Lifeguard Corps planned to double up on each station. When Bill came down to muster, he was told he was assigned to post number 17 alone. It was never that crowded, so he should be able to handle it. Bill headed to the truck, and as always, he was the last to be posted.

Bill had just gotten set up when he saw a bus loaded with boys and girls drive up. He knew at once it would be an exciting day. They came running towards the water like a herd of wild animals, hitting the water from every angle. Their adult leaders were right behind them. One came up and asked how the water was. He told him the water was up about two feet because of the tide and nor'easter. If they would watch for run outs, he didn't think there would be a problem.

About an hour later, the tide started to go out. You could see the run outs forming in the sand. About fifteen minutes later, Bill's fears materialized. He saw about twenty of the children playing in a run out. He blew his whistle and started down his chair. Then he heard the first scream.

"Help! Help! I can't stand up!"

Bill grabbed his buoy, threw down his flag, and started toward the run out. Then he heard another, "Help!" and another. As he got to the run out, he saw Lonnie. She had the child farthest out, so he started at the other end. In about ten minutes they had pulled ten people out. If Lonnie had not been there to help, he could not have saved them all. Bill was pulling the last one out when the truck arrived. The two adults with the group were counting heads. All were there, safe and sound.

The captain came up to Bill and asked, "How did you get them all out in time?"

Bill told him that without Lonnie, he couldn't have. The captain wanted to meet this Lonnie. But when they looked around, again she was gone. One of the adult leaders spoke up. "I don't know about any Lonnie, but this guy is one of the fastest lifeguards around. He swam faster than any Olympic swimmer getting to everyone. You all should be proud of him."

The captain put his hand on Bill's shoulder and said, "We are, we are!"

That night, Bill couldn't wait to get down to the beach to see Lonnie. She was sitting on the big rocks next to the bulkhead. He asked her why she would not stay so that he could introduce her to all the others. As long and as hard as she had worked to save those lives, she should get some of the credit. She just looked at him and smiled, but didn't say anything.

They walked down the beach a long time that night. They talked about nearly everything—their hopes, likes, and plans for the future. But when he asked her anything personal, she always changed the subject. She wouldn't tell him anything about her past. This puzzled Bill. She seemed to like him, but wouldn't go out with him or let him take her home to meet his family.

Bill saw Lonnie nearly every day that he worked on the lifeguard stations. At night, they would walk up and down the beach, always after nine o'clock.

Then came the biggest day for beachgoers: the Fourth of July. He had done so well that summer that he was promoted to a senior guard position and assigned to the boardwalk tower. That day, the boardwalk tower guards pulled sixteen swimmers to safety. Each time he went out for someone, Lonnie was there ahead of him, sometimes a little way off in the distance. The other guys teased him about his phantom girlfriend that he was always talking about, but whom no one had ever seen. That night he told Lonnie that he wanted her to sail with him the next day. She said that she would and maybe she could clear up some of the mysteries and questions he had—that is, if he would promise not to tell anyone about what she would show him. Bill promised.

The next day he got his outrigger and headed toward post 17. About halfway there, Lonnie came up alongside the boat. "Come aboard," Bill said.

"First, I must explain something. Go out to sea about a half mile, then throw out your sea anchor."

After they were out there, she asked, "Bill, have you ever heard of a sea nymph, a siren, or a mermaid?" He nodded. "Well, you see," she continued, "that's what I am."

"Ah, come on, don't pull my leg"

Lonnie said, "Okay, help pull me aboard."

As Bill pulled her from the water, her long hair fell over her breasts, which were covered with seaweeds. As he pulled her in farther, he could not see her swimsuit. As she came farther out of the water, Bill could see her below the waist. He became speechless, for just below her belly button, there was the most beautiful blue-green fish-tail he had ever seen—no legs, only a tail. He couldn't believe his eyes. His Lonnie was indeed a mermaid. All he could say was, "How?"

Then Lonnie told her story.

Many, many years ago when she was just a young girl, she had gone swimming in this area of tower 17 and had been caught in a run out. She was a Timucuan Indian princess. Just before she drowned, the mermaids of the lost continent of Atlantis found her. They turned her into a sea nymph to prevent her from drowning. The catch was that she had to help drowning people here until she found someone who would love her no matter what. When she did, she could live with him in the sea or on the land, whichever they chose.

She looked at Bill and added, "Do you love me like that, Bill?"

He held her close to him and said, "Yes, Lonnie, I do. But I have never lived in the water."

"Would you like to see what it's like for a few hours?"

"Sure," he said. "But how?"

Lonnie handed him a small blue-green pill. Bill took it, swallowed it, and in just a few moments felt a tingling in his legs.

"Take off your pants, quick!" Lonnie said. He did, just as a bright blue-green light covered his legs. When the light had gone, Bill also had a huge fishtail in the place of his legs.

"Follow me," she said, and dove into the water with Bill right behind her.

They played and swam nearly all day. Bill said it was a glorious feeling—he never seemed to tire and felt like birds must feel when they fly. Lonnie showed him many things and places he had only heard about in fairytales. When it was time to go up, she asked, "Well, what do you think?"

All Bill could say was "Great!" When they got back to the boat, he could feel his legs return. Lonnie swam away and waved back.

"I'll see you on the beach tomorrow night," she called.

Bill could hardly wait. The next night he was waiting for her as she came up out of the water. He saw the light and saw her fish tail turn into legs. As she walked toward him, he was amazed at how adaptable she was in the water and on the land. They sat together and talked for a while, then she asked, "Have you decided? Yes or no?"

Bill said, "Yes, I do love you and want to be with you, but I'm only sixteen. This is a decision I can't make right now."

Lonnie looked a little sad, but looked up at him and said, "I know you love me, Bill, and I didn't really expect you to decide now. See this little spot on my hip?" She pulled down her shorts so he could see. "When you are older, you will meet someone who will have a spot like this. I don't know how long it will be, but you will remember. Her name will be Jean, but she will be called Jeannie. Remember me then—it just may be me. No matter where you may be, I will be with you. You may not see me all the time, but I will be there with you. At night while on the sea, you may hear me call. Remember, you must not forget me, if we are ever to see each other again. I must leave you, Bill. The summer is over and you must return to school. We may meet again next summer, who knows?"

She kissed Bill and walked back to the ocean. Just before going under she turned, waved, smiled, and was gone.

Over the next few years, Bill said that he saw her now and then. He also said that he kept his promise. He would never forget his phantom on the beach.

I saw Bill at our fortieth class reunion not long ago, and met his wife. I hadn't seen him for over twenty-five years. She was pretty, with long brown hair and blue-green eyes. As he introduced her, I stood in amazement.

"Her name is Jean," he said, "but I call her Jeannie."

They both seemed very happy and in love. I couldn't help wondering if he remembered telling me the story so many years ago.

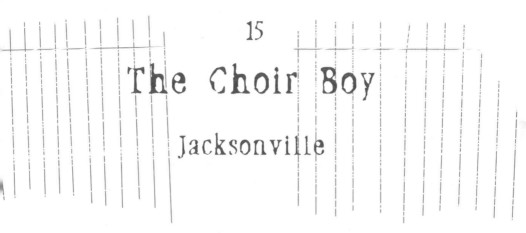

15

The Choir Boy

Jacksonville

Many years ago when I was a young boy, the youth in my church were told the story of the choir boy ghost of the Church of the Good Shepherd. At first, we didn't believe the story. We thought of it as something the older leaders of the church told the young people so we would be afraid to explore all of the secret passages and tunnels that were all over, under, and inside the church. It is about the biggest church in town. It had a great big Gothic cathedral, an indoor swimming pool and basketball court, an education building for Sunday school classes, and an auditorium with a stage for plays and musicals that were given quite often. This auditorium even had a balcony. The following story was told one night on a hayride.

Many years ago, not long after World War I, the church had just started its all-boy soprano choir and was in the process of building the indoor swimming pool. This was a beautiful pool for any era, but for that time it was unbelievable. It was about forty meters long and fifteen meters wide. It was completely tiled with small one-inch tiles up the wall for about ten feet. It had a balcony with three tiers and room for three rows of chairs on each level down one side. At the deep end of the pool was a one-meter diving board. In one corner of the deep end of the pool was a diving platform with two stations, one set at

75

m the water and the other at twenty feet.

...ny about half completed when the tale began. They were pouring concrete and connecting the tunnels used for the water pipes and drains. All of the boys were told to stay away from the area and to always stay out of the tunnels for fear they may get lost and no one would be able to find them.

There was one boy, about twelve or thirteen years old, whom they called "Baby Jimmy" because he had a baby face and sang like an angel. People would come from far away just to hear him sing on Sundays. Now, Jimmy may have had a beautiful voice and an angel face, but he did have a problem. He was very curious. If he was told not to do something, you could bet that would be the very thing he would do.

One Saturday after the boys had finished choir practice and had their drinks and cookies, they decided to play hide-and-seek. They had been told not to play near the pool construction for fear that some of them may get hurt, and of course you can guess the first place Jimmy went. That's right—to the pool construction area.

The boys played games on the patio of the church and in the Sunday school building most of the afternoon. When it was time to quit playing and go home, everyone was accounted for except Jimmy. All of the other boys and the adults looked everywhere for him. They even went over to the pool construction area and called for him, to no avail. When it began to get dark and families came to take their boys home, there was still no sign of Jimmy. The men of the church decided to get lamps and search the tunnels. One of the other boys had last seen him headed toward the pool area. He told him not to go, but Jimmy told him it was all right, that everyone worried too much and he just wanted to look around for a little while. That was the last time he had seen Jimmy.

The men searched and called for Jimmy all night long. The only thing they found was a piece of shirt in one of the tunnels under the choir loft and pipe organ. They also found one shoe over by the pool construction. They asked the construction workers to be on the lookout just in case they were to hear or see anything. All work on the pool area was stopped for well over a week.

Months later, the pool and gymnasium were completed, but no trace of Jimmy was ever found, nor was he ever seen or heard from again. That is, until the day before the pool was to open for swimming. The caretaker had finished the final coat of wax on the basketball court when he heard singing coming from the pool. He thought some of the choir boys had gotten in there earlier before it was opened. As he opened the door to the pool, he saw a choir boy standing on the diving board in his red robe and white smock, singing. He yelled at the boy and told him to get down from there, he had no business in there yet. As he turned to step over the rail, he looked up and the boy was gone. The caretaker thought that maybe he had had too much to drink the night before and was seeing things. He decided he wouldn't mention it to anyone.

Then, a day or two later, he was cleaning in the church when he heard someone playing the organ. He didn't think much about it at first but just thought that the choir master was practicing. As he got closer, he looked over at the organ. There, sitting at the organ, was the same choir boy that he had seen on the diving board. He spoke to the boy and asked him if he had permission to play the organ. The boy turned and looked straight at him for a few seconds. Then, right before his eyes, he watched the boy slowly fade away without a word.

This was all he could stand. He went straight to the minister's office and told him. Without saying a word more, the minister said that he would speak to the board members that night at their regular meeting.

The minister did as he had promised and mentioned the incident to the board. He was surprised at what he heard, for it seemed that the caretaker was not the only one who had seen the choir boy. The choir master had seen him twice—once playing the organ and another time in the pipe alley singing. The others told their stories of the choir boy. He had been seen a number of times down by the pool, and others had seen him as he disappeared into the doorway or into one of the secret passages. They even found openings to passages that had not been used for years that no one had even remembered existed. Many had heard the choir boy sing, but when they would get close enough to him to speak, he would either fade away or disappear into the passages.

Many believe it to be the ghost of Jimmy. Some said that his voice was identical, and those who saw him and had known Jimmy said that it was him without a doubt. Some believe that Jimmy's curiosity got the best of him that Saturday, and while exploring the tunnels, he had become lost in them somewhere or gotten hurt and, unable to call back to the searchers, he eventually died. Others believe that in trying to find a place to hide near the pool construction on that fateful Saturday, he had fallen into one of the holes dug for the pool supports and was killed. When the men poured the concrete, he was covered forever.

Over the years, many people claimed to have encountered this apparition of the choir boy, but most of us felt that it was just a story to keep all of us out of the tunnels—and it worked for the most part.

I first heard of the choir boy ghost when I was a teenager back in the 1940s, but it wasn't until 1957 that I first encountered the apparition. I wasn't a child then, afraid of what some people call ghosts; that evening I had stayed after the pool had closed so I could prepare for the swimming classes I was to teach the next day, and I heard someone singing at the other end of the pool. I peeked out the door to see if I could catch whoever it was. I could see a choir boy standing by the diving board singing. I yelled at him to come to the office right then, as he had no business out there. He just stood there and stared at me with a puzzled look on his face. I turned on the lights, and when I looked again, he was gone. I searched all around the area and could find nowhere that he could have gone without me seeing him. Then I remembered the story of the missing choir boy.

I had another encounter with this ghost about a year later. I was in my office getting ready to leave late one night after a swimming meet. I had just locked the door and was passing by the basketball courts when I heard girls screaming. I thought everyone had left, but I ran back inside and turned on the lights. There at the other end of the pool was Danny, an old high school friend who lived directly behind the church. He was a fine looking boy who loved and was loved by girls. Danny and two girls were standing down by the diving board. None of them had on any clothes. When the girls saw me, they ran to me, not caring if they had any clothes on or not. They huddled in my office, along with Danny, talking about what had happened. Not once did they notice their lack of clothing. After a bit, I gave them some towels to put around them while they told me everything.

They had decided to go skinny dipping with Danny that night. They climbed through the windows after everyone had gone home and waited until I turned off the lights and left before they took off all their clothes to go in the water. Just as they got everything off, they heard someone giggling over by the diving board. They looked and saw one of the choir boys, about twelve years old, standing in the shadows of the moonlight that was coming through the skylight windows. Danny ran toward him to scare him off, but just as Danny reached him, he started to fade away. Danny grabbed at him and his hand went right through him as though he wasn't there. That's when the girls screamed. They continued to scream until I got there and turned on the lights.

I went down and got their clothes from the other end of the pool since none of them would go after them. They all dressed right there in my office. This was surely one night none of us will ever forget. Many of Danny's friends never understood why he would not go back into the pool at night, but I knew. I had also promised him that I wouldn't tell and never did as long as he lived.

Not long after that I found a better paying job and moved away. I have often wondered if they still see the ghost of the choir boy now and then. I am sure they still tell his story, even if it is only to scare people away from going into those tunnels. But I know the truth of the ghost story, and so did Danny and those girls.

If by chance you do get to go by the church, be sure and look for Baby Jimmy at the pool. He may even sing for you.

16

The Old Fort

Fernandina

This tale was told not too many years ago by a camper at the state park at Old Fort Clinch. Here is his story, as told by him.

***

I had been many times to the old fort in Fernandina for various reasons. It's now a state park and has been for years. The park has picnic areas, nature trails, fishing, and a great historical tour. The fort is located at the mouth of the St. Marys River, which is the border between Georgia and Florida. It was built in the early part of the nineteenth century and was used fully through the Civil War and partially through the Spanish-American War. Now it is used only as a tourist attraction.

My story takes place in the mid 1960s, when I had taken my family camping at the park. Our camp was on the river, about 150 to 200 yards from the fort. We didn't want to camp on the ocean side because there was no shade and it was very hot during the day.

Late one afternoon, all of the day tourists—people who come down to the park only for the day and then go home—were all gone and only the campers were left in the park. I decided to take a walk

down by the jetties around the fort while my wife fixed supper. The jetty rocks were all the way around the fort. They had been brought in as ballast on some of the ships and placed around the fort to prevent beach erosion. As I went over the sand dunes, I saw a brilliant light.

I thought at first that someone had put a spotlight on me or set off a flash camera. As I approached the western side, from a distance I saw a man standing on the rocks by one of the big guns facing the river. As I approached him, I could see that he was in uniform. As I came even closer, I saw that it was a colonel's uniform. I decided that he must be a part of park services or maybe one of the tour guides. I walked up to the side of the rock he was standing on and spoke to him. He turned to me and seemed a bit startled. He returned my greeting in what seemed to be a Virginian accent with just a touch of British in it. He was a very distinguished looking gentleman, one could almost say aristocratic, without being a snob. He had dark hair with just a hint of gray in it and a black mustache. His uniform was impeccable, everything in its place. I'm not very good at guessing ages, but I would guess he was in his late forties. He asked me if I was one of the new recruits. I told him no, that I was just there camping with my family, and asked him why he had asked. He told me I was dressed so differently than the rest that he thought I must be one of the locals. I told him that I was a local, but I had nothing to do with the fort at the park. I was only camping over on the other side of the dunes. He then started to talk about the fort. He was on an inspection tour for General Scott of all the forts south of Washington and in the Gulf areas. I thought to myself, "For one of those re-enactors, this guy is really good. I haven't seen anyone so wrapped up in their job since the last time I visited Williamsburg, Virginia." I let him continue because I was really enjoying this.

I walked with him around the fort for about an hour. He explained to me the setup of the area, and why this fort was so important if we should ever be attacked again like we were in the War of 1812 with the British. I thought to myself, "This guy is really great at this."

There was something about him that seemed familiar, but I knew that I had not seen him before. He knew his history for this area, and in fact for all of the United States, up until the mid 1800s. He told me that the men at the fort were a little too lax; they too easily trusted the ships and schooners that came by. He said this could be the downfall of the fort someday if this didn't change and they did not become a little more conscious of security. He finally said that he had seen all that he thought he needed to see and must go for now, as he had to dispatch his notes to Washington by morning. I asked him his name before we parted. He turned back to me and said, "Robert, if you should ever want to join this army, tell them I sent you. We need all the bright young men we can get nowadays. Many of our finest are moving west."

I told him that I would remember his name since mine was Robert, too. I really don't know what it was, but I still felt that there was some-thing very familiar about this man. Maybe it would come to me.

After he had gone, I turned back to our campsite. I looked over my shoulder as Robert entered the fort. Another man, also dressed like a soldier, opened the gate to let him in. As the gate opened, I could see other men inside dressed as soldiers sitting around their fires eat-ing. Some of the men snapped to attention when Robert went by. It did seem very strange to me that these re-enactors could take the act-ing so seriously. I had heard men talking and could even smell food cooking on the open fires. Voices carry quite well near the water. As I got to the top of the dune, I saw that flash of light again. As my eyes adjusted to the bright light, my first thought was that it was probably going to rain.

Early the next morning, I got up and started a fire for breakfast. After we had all eaten and cleaned up the dishes, we decided to walk over to the old fort and see how the actors were doing.

When we got to the gate of the fort, I asked about the re-enactors. The gatekeeper looked at me like I had lost my mind. He said there wasn't any of that going on that he knew anything about. The last thing he remembered was about fifteen years ago when Gary Cooper made a movie about the Seminoles and their massacre of Colonel Dade's men. I thanked him and we went in. Inside, the fort was empty. There were no soldiers, camps, or fires, nor could we see where they had been the night before. There was only one old park ranger, dressed in brown. But I knew that I hadn't dreamed it all.

The children and I spent all day hiking through the woods, swim-ming, fishing, and eating. After supper, I told them I was going to take another walk over near the fort. Again, as I started out over the sand dunes, I was hit by that brilliant burst of light.

As I approached the fort, again I could hear voices coming from the gate.

There at the gate stood a soldier. I think it was the same one who had been there the previous night. I waved to him and he returned my greeting, but nothing was said. I walked around the side of the fort facing the ocean, and there on the jetties stood Robert, looking out to sea.

I approached him and spoke. "You look a little troubled, Robert. Is anything wrong?"

He said, "No, I was just wondering what is going to happen if this nation should go to war."

I decided to go along with the joke. "Well, Robert," I said. "When Mr. Lincoln is elected President, we will have a great Civil War. This fort will be taken by the North in eighteen-sixty-two by gunboats that come in flying a British flag. Then in nineteen hundred, we will go to war with Spain. This war will be called the Spanish-American War. In nineteen-seventeen, there will be another great war in Europe with Germany and Turkey. They will call it the Great War to End All Wars, but it was not. History will eventually call that war the First World War. In nineteen-forty-one, we will go to war again. This time we will fight Germany, Italy, and Japan. This war will be called the Second World War. In nineteen-fifty, we will have what they call a Police Action in Korea. This action will kill more men than the Civil War of the eighteen-sixties did on both sides. This Korean action will also be called The Forgotten War. Then there will be Vietnam. This will be called The Politicians' War and the Unpopular War."

I paused and looked at Robert, who was looking at me with an expression of disbelief. I said, "Hey! We are kidding, aren't we?"

He continued to stare at me for a few moments, then he said, "Son, how do you know these things? Especially this Mr. Lincoln. I have heard of Mr. Lincoln of Illinois. Is this the same man?"

"Yes, it is! He will be elected President in eighteen-sixty. That's when we have the Civil War, when the North and the South split."

"How do you know this?"

I must have looked a little startled at the shock I saw on his face. Something told me that he wasn't joking. I said, "I know this from our history books, of course."

Some of the shock left his face, and he started to ask some questions. "Tell me a little about this Civil War you spoke of."

I looked him in the eyes and decided to continue the game. I told him all about the Civil War—how it started, when it started, what it was fought over, and why. I told him all about the North's great leaders, what had happened here in Fernandina and how my great grandfather led the Fourth Florida Volunteers who were stationed here when it was taken. I went into details about how Fort Clinch was taken and how the Confederates almost got cut off getting away, then I started on the great battles in northern Virginia and of the south's greatest leader, Robert E. Lee.

At this point he stopped me and said, "Robert, you really do have quite an imagination, don't you?" He looked at me very intently and asked, "You aren't joking, are you, Robert?"

"No, but I believe that you are."

"Robert, tell me what year this is that you believe you are in right now."

I looked into his face knowing that he was dead serious. I responded, "Why it's nineteen-sixty-six, of course!"

He took a step back and said, "You aren't kidding, are you?"

"No!" I replied, "Why?"

"This is not nineteen-sixty-six, Robert. It is eighteen-fifty-six."

I started to laugh a little and said, "You aren't kidding, either, are you?"

He asked me to come inside with him for a little while and then said, "I have something to show you and many questions to ask."

We went through the main gate. The guard at the gate said, "Good evening, Colonel. Did you have a nice walk?"

Robert answered him and said, "This young man is coming in with me for a cup for coffee, then he will be leaving. I would like for him to have free access to me and the fort."

As we walked into the courtyard, it looked very different and newer than it had that morning. All of the big guns looked almost new. There were barracks and other buildings inside that had not been there earlier in the day. In fact, there had only been foundations for the building that now stood. None of this had been there before.

Robert took me to the officers' quarters and had his orderly pour us a cup of coffee. Then he said, "I don't know for sure what has happened or why, but it seems to me that you have come back in time, over a hundred years, if I'm not mistaken. I want to ask a few questions, then I will show you something. I want to ask first some questions about this General Robert E. Lee from Virginia of whom you spoke."

We sat for hours talking. I told him everything I knew about Lee and the Civil War—where he went to school, how well he did at West Point Military Academy, all about his escapades in the Mexican War, where his Virginia home was before the Civil War. When I had finished, he just sat for a minute in what seemed to be a daze.

Then he spoke. "This is just unbelievable, but you are absolutely right about everything that has happened so far."

"Do you know General Lee?" I asked.

He looked at me again and said, "Yes, I believe I know the man you are talking about quite well."

"I wish I could have known him."

He said, "You do, Robert, but he's not a general." He then turned to a packet of papers on the table, and handing them to me, said "Take a look at these."

The packet was addressed to Colonel Robert E. Lee and it was from the Inspector General's Office. I looked at him and opened the packet. Inside were orders to inspect the forts on the east coast of the United States and the Gulf of Mexico.

This time I was the one in shock. I looked up at him and said, "Your name is Robert E. Lee?"

He said, "Yes, I am Robert."

We sat and talked together for most of the night. Then I told him that I had better try to get back to my tent. He put his hand on my shoulder and told me how glad he was that we had met, but that he truly hoped that he was dreaming and that this nation would not go to war with itself. We clasped hands in farewell. I told him that I wished that it had been a dream, too, but the things I had told him were true. As I held his hand, I could feel the concern in his voice. I know now what this man had felt during the Civil War. He truly was deeply concerned about people. One would follow this great man through hell if he asked it. We waved goodbye to each other. As I reached the top of the dune, there was again another burst of bright light. I knew that I was back in my own time and place.

When I got back to my campsite, my wife met me. "Where have you been? I was about to call for the park rangers to go look for you."

I told her that she wouldn't believe me if I told her, then said that I was over at the fort and had fallen asleep.

The next morning we packed up to head for home. I wanted to get away before the other tourists and picnickers started to arrive. As we left, I looked over at the old fort. It was again an old fort, not the one I had visited the night before. I knew I wouldn't tell anyone about this. They wouldn't believe me anyway.

A few weeks later, I had the opportunity to be in the main public library in downtown Jacksonville. While browsing through the history of Florida, the name "Fort Clinch" seemed to jump out at me. It was just one line. It said, "Colonel Robert E. Lee had visited Fort Clinch in 1856 while on an inspection tour of all southern forts." I remembered that Colonel Lee had told me the same thing about why he was there at that time.

After reading, I went to the *Volumes on the War of the Rebellion* and looked up Fort Clinch, Fernandina, Florida. The book told all about the fort's capture in 1862 by the Federal gunboats. At the end of the chapter was a copy of a letter (or order) from General Robert E. Lee to General Finnigan, Fort Clinch, Florida. It said the following:

"As you know, sir, I made an inspection tour of your fort as directed by the then General of the Army of the United States, Winfield Scott. My orders were to insure that all of our forts along the Atlantic and Gulf Coast be brought up, or kept up in War Readiness, in case there may be a war. At that time it was brought to my attention, from a very reliable source, how the fort could or would be taken should there be a war. I must at this time insist that you show extreme caution in dealing with unknown ships, should they enter your harbor, especially if they should be flying the British flag and the year be 1862. These precautions should not be considered suggestions, but instead, they are Direct Orders."

It was signed by Robert E. Lee, General Commanding, The Confederate States of America and was dated January 1862.

I then knew that he had believed me. I also knew how he seemed to always stay one step ahead of the Northern armies in Virginia. He may have gotten the knowledge from me as to what would happen, but no one could have given him the compassion that he felt for his men and his home state of Virginia, and indeed the rest of the South. Robert E. Lee was not only the greatest general of his time, but no man was ever loved or respected more by his men. They did indeed follow him through hell. The hell was called the American Civil War.

I read a little further into the papers. Lee was once interviewed by a reporter after the war, while he was President of Washington College in Virginia. He was asked by the reporter how he seemed to always know where the enemy would be and what he needed to do to win. He said he had been told by a very good friend named Robert a long time ago and he wrote it down, at least all he could remember. He had indeed given me credit.

I will always be proud to have known him personally. I know not why I was chosen to walk through time and talk with him. Maybe it was fate that I was lucky enough to find that doorway, or maybe a greater power had a reason for me to find it. I may never know why! I may even try again someday to find that doorway through time to see what another time and place has to offer. There are many other great people of the past that I would like to meet in person.

17

The Pirate

Little Talbot Island

For centuries Florida has been known and recognized as having been a haven for pirates during the fifteenth through the eighteenth centuries. The Spanish built a fort in St. Augustine to protect their ships, which were loaded with gold and silver from the Yucatan for their king. Even today there are pirates moving contraband to and from Florida for many different reasons, in and around the state.

This story, as told to me by a friend, takes place around 1948 while he was on a family picnic on Little Talbot Island, which is located between Jacksonville and Fernandina.

***

I had finished eating and couldn't go back into the water for another hour so I wouldn't get cramps. I was walking around the sand dunes about half a mile down the beach from the rest of my party and sat down looking out over the Atlantic Ocean, thinking about what it must have been like for those explorers who first came there. As I sat there, I thought I heard some people in the sand dunes about fifty feet ahead. I got up and walked over to where the sounds were coming from. As I approached, the voices got louder and louder and as I

91

peeked over the second dune, I saw them.

They were surly and dressed funny and looked like the pictures I had seen of pirates. Then, all of a sudden, they started to argue and fight. One of the men pulled out a knife and stabbed one of the others in the chest. The other man took his sword and stabbed it all the way through the third man, then he finished covering the hole they had dug. As he finished, another pirate came up over the other side of the sand dune. This one was really a beauty. He was dressed completely in black from head to foot. He had on a very large coat, and in his belt he had two flintlock pistols and a sword. On his head he had a wide-brimmed hat with one big, white feather sticking out of it. His hair was so black that it seemed to shine and glow. His raven-black beard was braided into ten braids, with a purple ribbon tied at the end of each of them. He was about the meanest looking man I have ever seen. I had been watching the two men for about ten minutes when they started to argue about something. I couldn't make out what they were arguing about from where I was hiding, but their accents sounded British. Then, all of a sudden, the man with the black hair and beard pulled out one of his pistols and shot the other man in the head. He reached down, picked up the shovel, threw a few shovels of dirt on the man he had shot, and walked away.

I then rolled over in the sand so I couldn't be seen and looked up at the sky, thinking that I must be dreaming. I couldn't believe what I had just seen. After a while, I rolled back over to see if the man in black was still there. He was gone! I could see where the pirates had dug, and could even see a leg sticking out of the sand. As I was looking, I felt something pointed touch me between the shoulders. Rolling back over, I saw the man in black standing over me, with his cutlass just inches from my throat.

At first the man didn't say anything, and after what seemed like forever, he spoke in a deep, resonating voice with a definite British accent, "What are you doing here, laddie? Are you a castaway or what?"

After finally finding my voice, I said, "I was only walking on the beach, sir."

He looked at me as though he didn't believe me. I wasn't sure I believed me either. "What's your name, lad?"

"James, sir!"

"Good!" he said. "At least you're British."

"No, sir!" I said. "I'm American."

He looked puzzled. "American? What's an American?"

Before I could answer him, he said, "Do you know who I am?"

"No, sir!" I said.

He put his hand out to help me up. "My name is Teach, Captain

Edward Teach. To some I am known as Blackbeard." He looked hard at me and said, "Now, what am I to do with you? If I maroon you here, you'll surely die. If I take you with me, you'll tell what you have seen. I'll have to think on this one."

He sat down beside me and we talked for well over an hour. I told him all about myself and how I came to be there. I don't think he really believed me, though. After we talked he turned to me and said, "Laddie, I'm going to leave you here, being that's what you seems to want me to do."

He told me all about how he became a pirate and why. I had already forgotten about the killings on the sand dunes. He didn't seem nearly as fearsome as I had thought at first. Captain Teach explained to me the law of the pirates, and why they had kept their hiding place secret. He reached into his pocket before he left and handed me a coin. "Take this doubloon, lad. I don't know where you will spend it, but it will help you to remember me now and then."

I thanked him and reached into my pocket, found a half dollar, and handed it to him. I watched as the long boat came through the mist to pick him up. He climbed into the boat and waved goodbye to me as they pulled away. I could barely see his ship out beyond the breakers, but I could see the three masts and high afterdeck.

I turned to go back up the beach to where the family was. I hadn't gone far when the mist cleared and the bright sun came out. I had walked for a little way when I saw some of my family headed my way. They had walked up and down the beach looking for me and wanted to know where I had been. I just told them that I had been walking to help settle my lunch. I knew I couldn't tell them what had really happened. No one would believe it anyway.

I reached down into my pocket to feel the coin Blackbeard had given me. I'll show it to them someday, if the time is ever right. But for now it will be my secret. They would just think I had fallen asleep on the beach. I would think so, too, if I didn't still have this coin, I thought to myself.

A few years later, I went to the library to find something to read for a book report. As I wandered down the rows of books, I happened to see one sticking out about two inches. I pulled it from the shelf and read the title: *Blackbeard the Pirate.* As I opened the book, there on the second page was a painting of the pirate I had talked to on the beach. Under the picture it read, "Captain Edward Teach, also known as Blackbeard. One of the most infamous pirates to plague the east coast of Florida and the Gulf of Mexico."

I checked the book out and took it home. I wanted to examine the picture a little more closely. I took out my magnifying glass as soon as I got in the house and looked at the medallion around his neck. Sure enough, in the medallion was the coin I had given him on the beach.

I have thought about it many times over the years, and I am convinced that somehow on the beach, on that day, and at that time, I stepped through a time warp and met Blackbeard the pirate as he and some of his men were burying some of his stolen treasure. I have gone back to that site and dug a number of times trying to see if I could find his treasure, but to no avail. He may have come back for it later.

Others have looked at the picture of Blackbeard and say they can't tell if it is a half dollar for sure, because it's just a painting and a little blurred. But it does look a little like one. To me it really doesn't matter, though, because I know what it is. I gave it to him, and I have the doubloon he gave to me.

18

The House
on the Hill

Green Cove Springs

When I was a young boy of about twelve or thirteen, my family and I lived on Black Creek, which is located about six miles north of Green Cove Springs, Florida, on what was called the Hybernia Route. About half a mile up an old dirt road, on a bluff overlooking the St. Johns River and the entrance to Black Creek, was a big, two-story, wood-frame house. The old house must have been beautiful in its day. It had a very large front porch that you could sit on and see anything moving up or down the river. When I first saw it, though, the old house was pretty run down. Most of the windows on the house were broken and cobwebs now hung in place of the glass. The paint was chipped, baring pieces of rotted wood, and the grass had long ago been overtaken by weeds.

Living so far back in those woods, I was pretty lonesome staying home on weekends. There were no other children to play with. Dad didn't come home on weekends very often and my sister usually stayed much of the time in Jacksonville with some of her friends. Most of the time, then, I would just walk up the old dirt road to the house on the hill. I didn't think anyone lived there because it seemed so very run down. So I would go up and sit on the porch and daydream about the

people who had once lived there, wondering what may have become of them.

Then one summer day, while I was sitting on the porch in deep thought, I thought I saw something move over at the other end of the porch. I got up and walked over that way to see what it was. Just as I got to the edge of the porch, I saw a boy run out behind the shed on the other side of the house. I yelled to him to stop and wait for me, but when I got to the shed no one was there. I called to him to come back, but I didn't see or hear anything.

When I went home that afternoon, I asked Mama if she knew of anyone else living in this area. She told me that she didn't and that she hadn't heard Jim, the old black man who kept a garden out by our place, say anything about anyone. She did tell me, though, that she would ask him the next time he came by.

I woke up early the next day because I wanted to go back up to the old house in hopes that I would see that boy again. It got so lonely out there with no one to play with, and I was excited about the possibility of finding a playmate. I had been sitting on the porch for quite some time and had almost forgotten the boy I had seen yesterday, when out of the corner of my eye I saw someone peeking at me around the corner of the porch. I called out, "Hi there!" When the person pulled back, I could hear someone run down the side porch. I called, "Please don't run away. Stay and talk to me for a little while. I won't bother you."

When I got to the end of the porch, there standing very still but looking straight at me, was a young girl of about twelve. I spoke to her, "My name is Robert!" She started to turn and go. "Please don't go!" I said. "Stay and talk a little, please. Come up here on the porch."

She took a few steps towards me and stopped. I could see that she was about my age. I don't think I have ever seen a prettier girl in all my life. She had long, light brown, curly hair that reached past her waist, and she had a few yellow bows tied in the back of it. Her dress was long, reaching almost to her ankles, and was light blue. An apron was tied securely around her waist with a big bow in the back, and she had on high button shoes. She just stood there for a little while looking at me, not saying anything.

I told her again, "My name is Robert. What's yours?"

Very softly she said, as if she didn't expect me to hear her, "Jeannie."

I asked her if she lived near here. She answered, "Yes, here."

"Oh," I said, "you mean near here?"

"No, right here."

"But I didn't think anyone lived in this old house. How long have you lived here?"

"Oh, we've been here a long, long time."

I asked her if it was her that I saw yesterday.

She told me, "No, that was my brother Andrew."

Jeannie stayed and talked with me for well over an hour, then she said that she had to go for now. I asked her if she would come back tomorrow and talk with me again. She promised that she would come if she could.

All the way home I just skipped and talked to myself about Jeannie. I had a crush on her already, and it was bad. I couldn't help it, but at least I had someone to talk to. I told Mama about Jeannie and Andrew. She just said that she was glad that I had found someone to play with.

The next day, I was at the old house early. I knocked on the door this time to let Jeannie and Andrew know I was there, but no one seemed to be at home. I felt a cold chill, and I was afraid Jeannie and Andrew had gone and I wouldn't see them again. I sat on the steps for a while waiting. When I started to leave, I looked down the porch. There stood Jeannie and Andrew.

"Hi!" I said, "I didn't hear you come up. I thought no one was at home. I knocked on the door."

Jeannie said, "I'm sorry. We were down on the dock playing. We do spend time down there quite often."

We talked for a long time and we played hide-and-seek for a bit, then Jeannie said they would have to go for now, but would be back tomorrow.

I spent every day down at the old house with Jeannie. Sometimes we walked down by the river holding hands. Most of the time Andrew was with us, or not far away.

The summer was now coming to an end. I had planned to spend a few weeks with my aunts, which I did every summer. I didn't want

Jeannie, but I knew that I had to go.

﹍all never forget my last day with Jeannie. We sat on a blanket up on the bluff holding hands.

Jeannie said to me, "Robert, please don't forget me. I'll never forget you."

I told her not to worry, as I could never forget her, and that I would be back in a couple of weeks anyway. She smiled at me, then reached over and kissed me and told me goodbye. I walked down the old dirt road backwards so I could see her as long as I could. She and Andrew waved to me as long as they could see me.

The next day I caught the bus and went to Gainesville. While I was there, Mama wrote and told me that Dad had found us a place in Jacksonville to live and we would be living there when it was time to come home.

I wrote to Jeannie many times while in Gainesville and after I got back to Jacksonville. All my letters were returned to me marked, "Return to Sender, Person and Address Unknown."

Years went by, then one day in the library, I found a book on the history of the area of Hybernia. As I was reading, I discovered a section about an ex-governor's old plantation home before and during the Civil War. This caught my interest right away, so I had to look into it a little further.

As I read some of the governor's old letters that were written during the Civil War, the names Jeannie and Andrew seemed to jump off the page at me. I read the letter fully, and this is what it said: "Dear Mama, I was hurt to hear about Jeannie's and Andrew's tragedy. Bryan said that they had been hiding out under the dock when some Yankees came ashore, but he didn't say how they died! What happened?"

I read on and on, but was unable to find any further mention of either Jeannie or Andrew. I was very confused at this point because I knew that it couldn't be the same Jeannie and Andrew I had known.

Finally, I decided to make a trip out to the old house on the hill once more. I had never heard anything from Jeannie, but I couldn't get her out of my mind.

First, I went to old Jim's house and asked him if he knew anything. He told me that no one had lived in that old house for over sixty years. He couldn't remember his old daddy saying anything, but his grand-daddy told him about the old house. He had been a slave there. He could remember him telling the young ones about the house being haunted by two children. This is how he remembered the story:

"They had hid the children out under the dock when the Yankees came for fear of what they may do. As the Yankees came closer, the boy got excited and fell into the water. When the little girl tried to save him, she lost her balance and fell into the water. They both drowned in the swift currents there at the bend in the river. Their little bodies were never found. Some folks claimed to have seen those two children playing around the old house."

I thanked him as I walked on down the old dirt road to the house on the hill. I hadn't been up this way for over fifteen years.

As I walked around the bend, there stood the old house just as I remembered it. I walked over to the bluff where we had played so often and where I had last seen Jeannie. I stayed there most of the day just thinking and remembering before starting for home. I remem-bered telling Jeannie all those years ago that I would never forget her, and I haven't.

As I started to leave, something made me take one last look. As I did, there standing in the same spot I had last seen them, stood Jeannie and Andrew. They were waving to me. I turned and started back. As I did, they started to fade away. I could see a tear in Jeannie's eye. I stopped and called to her with tears in my eyes. They seemed to understand. Then they smiled and waved once more to me as they faded away. I knew then that this would be the last time I would ever see them in this life.

To my knowledge, no one has ever encountered them again on the bluff or in the House on the Hill.

19

The Fog

St. Augustine

The night was clear, still a bit chilly and damp, but that wasn't really unusual for that time of year, as St. Augustine is so close to the ocean and Matanzas Inlet. I had heard many ghost stories about places in and around St. Augustine all my life, but paid very little attention to them. I had always thought of ghosts as things people not right in their minds saw and believed in. This story has been told for a long time in the area and this is the way it was told to me.

That night in February 1939 was not unlike this one, but it changed many people's outlook and belief in ghosts, including mine. It seemed that George, a young man of about seventeen with nothing better to do, decided to walk down by the old Castillo de San Marcos and on down by the place that was advertised as Ponce de Leon's Fountain of Youth. As George was on his way back and passing in front of the old fort on the inlet side, he looked out over the water and saw the heavy, dense fog as it rolled in from the ocean. There seemed to be something different about this fog. He had seen fog many times before, but none like this. This time it seemed much more eerie and silent. Then he realized what it was: the lack of sound coming from anything the fog passed. Everything was quiet, not a sound from a bird, dog, cat, cricket, frog, or anything. Very strange!

George stopped and watched as the fog came closer and closer. As it rolled across the inlet, passing the bell and other buoys, all sounds from them stopped as though a switch had turned them off. It made him think of the finger of death mentioned in the Bible when God sent his angel of death to Egypt to kill the firstborn. George stood in awe as the fog came closer and closer, until it was up to his feet, then his waist, and then he couldn't see a hand in front of his face.

It didn't bother him at first, but after a bit, the silence made him feel uneasy. As he turned back toward the direction of the fort, he stumbled over something. It felt as if something had grabbed hold of his foot. As he fell forward, he struck his head on one of the rocks around the fort sea wall. It stunned him, but he never lost consciousness. He lay there for a moment to shake the cobwebs from his head.

Then, through the fog, he heard voices. It sounded like men and women laughing and talking. As the voices came closer, he could tell that they were speaking Spanish. He didn't speak Spanish very well, but could pick out a word now and then. George pulled himself up and took a couple of staggering steps. Then someone took him by the arm; he turned to see who it was. There, holding his arm, was the most beautiful young girl he had ever seen. She seemed to be about his age. Her hair was raven black and she had very dark eyes and lashes, but he could see them sparkle. She spoke, "Señor, señor, are you all right?"

He could only stand there and look at her as she spoke again.

"Señor! Are you all right? I see you have fallen and hurt your head. Come over here and let me clean the cut for you."

He followed her over to one of the rocks and sat down. She took the corner of her scarf, dipped it into a small pool of water, and washed the blood from his forehead. The salt water stung a little, but in a moment it felt better.

She tried to speak to him in Spanish, but he told her that he didn't speak Spanish. She had no difficulty talking to him in English after that. They talked for a long while. She told him that her name was Lorina Cordova. She was dressed in the period dress of seventeenth-century Spain. He thought nothing of this because many of the shop owners dressed this way for the effect it had on tourists coming to the nation's oldest city.

George was captivated by the way she spoke. One could indeed think that she had come from the early Spanish occupation of Florida. He asked her about her family, where she came from, and where she was living now, and he told her that he would like very much to see her again.

Lorina told him that her family had come to this country from Castile, Spain, about six months ago, and that she was now living in the fort with her father, who was captain of the watch.

This surprised him, and he told her that he didn't think anyone lived at the fort, or had since the Civil War. Now she seemed surprised. She said that she knew most of the stories about this area, but had never heard of a Civil War.

After talking for a while longer, Lorina told him that she had better go in before her father came looking for her; if he should find her talking to an Englishman, he would really be upset.

As she started to go, George took her hand and kissed it. He asked her if he could see her again. At first she said no, then took hold of his hand and said, "Be here tomorrow night about this same time, and I will meet you here." She kissed him on the cheek, turned, and ran off into the fog.

The next day, all he could think of was his Lorina. He could hardly wait until the coming evening.

As George sat on the rock looking out across the water, it started to get dark. Still no Lorina, but he continued to wait. As it got later, he began to think that she wasn't coming.

Just as he was about to leave, he saw the fog coming in across the inlet. It covered everything and again he couldn't see anything. Then something made him turn around, and as he did, there stood his beautiful Lorina. He asked her what had taken her so long that night. All she said was, "I had to wait for the fog."

George and Lorina met like that for many nights during the next few months. Then Lorina stopped coming and George began to wonder and worry.

He skipped school the next day, thinking he would go visit the old fort. Maybe, just maybe, he could at least get a glimpse of her. He searched all over the fort for some sign of her, but there was nothing. Finally, he asked one of the park rangers and was told that he must be mistaken because it has been almost a hundred years since anyone actually had lived in the fort.

George was really downhearted. Why had Lorina lied to him? It had to have been because of her father.

Many years went by—even the Second World War had come and passed—but George never forgot Lorina. Then one evening as he sat on the bulkhead by the fort, he had a strange but familiar feeling as he watched the fog roll in across Matanzas Bay. As everything got quiet and the fog engulfed him and everything around him, George first smelled that same vanilla perfume from long ago.

Turning, there she stood above him on the parapet on the wall on the fort. George jumped up and started to run to her. Just before he got to her, she held up her hand for him to stop. He heard her say, "Go to Maria's house. All of your answers will be found there." Then the fog covered the top of the wall and she was gone.

George got up early the next morning. Not knowing where to go, he decided to go to the St. Augustine Historical Society located in the building behind the oldest house. He went the lady there what he was looking for. She smiled at him. "Young man, this is your lucky day." He was astonished and asked her why.

"Because this old house was Maria's house. Now, come upstairs with me and we'll see what other information we can find on your Lorina Cordova."

As he came to the top of the stairs, he stopped dead in his tracks. There, hanging on the wall, was a painting of Lorina.

"That's her, that's the girl at the top of the wall!"

"But that can't be. She died over two hundred years ago. Come. I think I have a copy of that story."

She handed him a very old book. Printed in 1880, its edges were frayed and the pages had turned brown. He took the book to the end of the table and began to read:

"Our strange apparition has appeared once more on the upper walls of the old fort. It seems she appears only during the nights we have very heavy fog. This time she was seen by four people as they strolled the river bank. She is always reported to be looking for something or someone. This time they got close enough to recognize her as the ghost of Lorina Cordova.

"As the story goes, Lorina was very much in love with an Englishman she had met at the base of the fort. She had asked her father to allow her to see him again, but he made arrangements for her to marry a Spanish nobleman, whom she despised because of his arrogance and cruelty to those under him. On the night she was to be married, she climbed to the highest part of the fort's walls and dove off onto the rocks. She was dead before anyone found her. Her ghost or apparition has been seen by many people for well over a hundred years. There is no record of her having spoken to anyone. She just stands there looking out across the water for her Englishman."

George sat there stunned for what seemed like a long time. After a while, the curator of the society came by and told him that she had to close up for the night. George thanked her and left. He had only one intention, and that was to go down by the old fort and wait until Lorina came. He knew that she would.

For the next few weeks, a massive search was made for the man seen sitting on the rocks the night of the heavy fog, but it seems he was never found. Some claimed to have seen Lorina and her Englishman standing on the walls of the fort at night as the fog would come in. After talking with the people in the Historical Society, the belief is that Lorina did indeed come for him in the fog. It has been almost sixty years since George was last seen, except if you would like to count those who claimed to see the two ghosts of the fog.

20

Casa Monica

St. Augustine

My story begins in February in the year 2000. The old original Casa Monica, whose name was changed in the early 1900s to the Cordova Hotel and then renamed Casa Monica Hotel. The hotel was built to luxurious standards in 1888 and it has since been restored and refurbished to those original standards once again. The new owners have done a magnificent job in their restoration of the old hotel. It has many of the original Spanish-style furnishings. Also many of the original hand-painted Spanish tiles have been restored. The outside of the old hotel was restored as it had been in the 1880s; to look at it, a person would think it had just been built. All five of the original towers have been restored to the elegant suites they once were. The majestic corner tower is a luxurious three-story penthouse featuring two spacious bedrooms with panoramic views of the ancient town, beautiful Matanzas Inlet, and the Atlantic Ocean.

As I toured the corner tower for the first time, I had an unusual feeling. Everything seemed so familiar to me. I felt as though I had been there before, but I knew that I hadn't. It had been many years since it had been a hotel, way before my time anyway. As I walked I seemed to know exactly what would be in the next room, or around the next corner. How could this be?

We continued on our tour of this grand place. It truly was a castle. I had the feeling that I had indeed stepped back in time to this hotel's grand opening in the 1880s. It was no wonder to me that when it first opened, this hotel had hosted privileged clientele. From kings, presidents and lords of industry to authors, artists and Broadway stars—they gathered at this and other Flagler resorts. I had visited many other old Flagler hotels, but this one seemed so different, more like home, and something drew me to it.

As we finished our tour and were starting to leave we passed the original stairway. I don't know what made me look, but as my eyes followed the hallway and up the stairs, I saw a beautiful young lady standing on the first landing. She had long, light brown hair that flowed down to her shoulders. Her dress was a dark green color, with a high neck piece topped with lace, flowing with wide pleats down to the floor. It had long sleeves, bellowed at the shoulders and capped at the wrist with lace. Around her neck she wore a Greek cameo. (This also seemed familiar.) As she took a step down, I could see that she had on high button shoes. Her face was beyond beauty. Her eyes were large and bright. Her lips were small but full, with just a hint of color.

I know I must have seemed a fool as I stood there and stared at her as she descended the stairs. As she came within reach, I automatically put out my hand to assist her. She smiled at me very graciously and took my hand. Her hand was soft and warm. I knew that I knew her, but I just couldn't remember where we had met. She continued on to the lobby, as I stood there watching her go.

When I regained my senses and went on to the lobby, I looked around for her but she was nowhere to be seen. I even asked some of the others if they had noticed which way she had gone. I then went to the desk manager. I needed to find out who this girl in green was. I knew she had to work there from the way she was dressed. The manager didn't know who she was. He said that they had a few people in period dress, but he assured me that none of those dressed as elaborately as the lady I had described. I thanked him and went on with the tour, but I couldn't get her out of my mind.

Before leaving I made reservations to stay in the hotel for a couple of nights the next month.

I spent all of the month leading up to my stay in the Casa Monica reading everything I could find about the hotel and the people who had stayed there over the years since its grand opening. Had I only dreamed of this beautiful young lady who seemed so familiar to me? I had this feeling that if I didn't find out who she was I would never be happy. I asked every hotel employee I could find if they knew who she was, but no one seemed to know anything about her. I was beginning to think that I may have imagined her. Maybe she was from another tour, or maybe she was a ghost. I laughed at that one. The only ghost I had ever really believed in was the Holy Ghost that is mentioned in the Bible.

In March I arrived at the hotel. It was a beautiful day—not too cold or too hot. As I checked in, I glanced over towards the stairs, and to my amazement there she stood by the fountain looking straight at me. I walked over to her and spoke. "Good afternoon. I am so glad to see you again!"

"I'm glad to see you too," she said. "I really didn't think you would make it back so soon. But I am glad to see you. You go on and finish registering and I'll meet you in the dining room at seven, if that works with your plans."

Although a little astonished I said, "Great, I'll be there." I felt that I knew her, but I couldn't quite understand her familiarity. But I truly was glad for it. I wanted to get to know her better. I knew that I had only met her coming down the stairs on my last visit. But, like last time, she made me feel that I knew her quite well; but how? I wondered. Maybe she could help me find the answers at dinner.

I finished registering and was taken to my rooms by the bellhop. He showed me the closet and informed me that the management would like for us all to dress in period costume of the 1880s and 1890s if we would be so kind. I thanked him and told him that I would be happy to. I also told him that I was meeting a young lady for dinner at seven and would she be in costume too?

"But of course, sir! Miss Browne and her friends are expecting you at seven."

I had about two hours to get ready. I was very anxious to see what this was all about.

After cleaning up before dinner, I lay back on the couch and wondered about where I may have met this Miss Browne. She seemed to know me so well As I lay there I couldn't help but feel that I knew her—but from where? And when? I must ask her at dinner. Where could a beautiful young woman have met an old man in his late sixties? I knew that I would have remembered her.

I lay there for a short time and got up to look out the window at the park and old market place. At first I thought there was something different about the park. Then it came to me—the streets were lime rock and oyster shell, and all I could see were horses and buggies going up and down. But there seemed to be fewer people then I would have expected for a weekend. I guessed they were preparing for another celebration.

I finished dressing and went down to the lobby. All of the bellhops and other employees greeted me as I passed. "Good evening, Mr. Rogero," they would say to me and graciously I would return their greeting. I walked up to the maitre d', who said, "Follow me Mr. Rogero, your table is ready. Miss Browne is already there, but your other guests have not arrived yet."

"Thank you," I said as I followed him.

He led me to my table. Dora was sitting there alone. She was radiant in her light pink dress with its high ruffled neck and long sleeves. She looked as though she had stepped out of a catalogue of the 1890s. Very beautiful, I thought. But how did I know her name? It just seemed to come to me.

"Good evening, Miss Browne. You look exceptionally stunning tonight," I said as I tipped my hat.

Smiling, she reached out her hand to me. I took it and kissed the back of it.

"We are extremely formal tonight, aren't we, Mr. Rogero?"

I smiled and sat down beside her.

"I knew that you would come back, John! I have missed you this last year. Have you been writing anything? My students have asked me if I would have any more stories for them. I told them I would hope so, if you had finished any.

"What's wrong, John? You seem to be so way off somewhere. It's as if you aren't sure of yourself now."

"Well, Dora, I guess I'm in a daze. You see, I'm not sure of myself."

About that time another couple came up to our table. "John, I would like you to meet Bernie and Frances Munday. They are old friends from school. I've told them about your writing and have asked them to join us."

I stood up and shook Bernie's hand while bowing to Frances. "The pleasure is mine, I'm sure."

"Dora has spoken of you quite often, John. I'm glad you could make it back for the grand opening. I understand Mr. Flagler will be here. He has really made St. Augustine into a great resort city since he bought that old narrow-gauge railroad, the Jacksonville to St. Augustine, in eighty-three and widened it to standard. His new Florida East Coast Railroad is beginning to grow. We can all see what it is doing for Florida and St. Augustine, with these three grand hotels: the Casa Monica, the Alcazar, and now his great Ponce de Leon."

"Now Bernie, don't talk so much. We all know how proud you are of Mr. Flagler's new railroads," said Frances.

Bernie bowed his head and said, "I'm sorry, but it does make me proud to be a part of it all. I've been with him since eighty-three when he first started his railroad. Mr. Flagler's dreams are to run the railroad all the way to Key West someday."

"He will, too! You can put your money on it." I said.

"That's great, John. You are the first person I've mentioned it to that didn't think Mr. Flagler had lost his mind. Some are already call-ing it 'Flagler's Folly,' and he hasn't even begun to make plans yet."

"Don't worry, Bernie, let them all make their fun. You and Mr. Flagler will build your railroad to Key West."

"Dora, I really like this guy. He makes me feel as though he can see the future. His responses are so positive. You will let me present him to Mr. Flagler won't you?"

"Of course, Bernie," Dora said. "I think that would be a fine idea."

We smiled at each other as we began our dinner. I really couldn't tell whether she was catering to me or Bernie.

After dinner we sat and had coffee and tea while the orchestra set up. When they started to play, I asked Dora to dance with me as they started a Viennese Waltz.

"You really dance divinely, John. I didn't think you took time for this sort of thing."

After the waltz we stepped out onto the veranda for a breath of fresh air.

"What is it now, John?" she said. "You seem so different somehow."

"I'm not sure I know myself, Dora, and if I tell you, you will most likely think I have lost my mind."

"Tell me, John, please."

"I don't know where to start. But do you remember last month in the lobby, you nodded to me, while I was on the tour of the hotel?"

"I remember meeting you last year when they started building this hotel. That wasn't last month!"

I stepped back. "No jokes now, Dora, what year is this?"

"Why, John, you know this is January eighteen-eighty-eight."

"How did we meet?"

"We were introduced by our friends Mr. Weedman and Mr. Baya, the members of the school board. For the month you were here last year, we became quite close. Or have you forgotten that too?" she said a little angrily.

"No, Dora, I have been in love with you for many years, ever since

I saw your picture in the hotel lobby." How did I know that, I wondered.

"What hotel?"

"This one!"

"How can that be? This hotel has just opened and I assure you, my picture is not hanging in the lobby."

"But it will be. You see, I am from the year two thousand. Somehow I seem to have come back in time to be with you."

"This is ridiculous. If you don't want to be with me, just say so!"

"Please wait, Dora, and I'll try to explain as best I can. You see I am not from this time. I was born in nineteen-thirty-three, which is forty-five years from now. I would think that a beautiful young woman like yourself would not even notice an old man like me. I saw you for the first time in the year two thousand at the reopening of this grand hotel. I had taken a tour when I first saw you, even though I must admit I felt all along that I knew you. Anyway, I couldn't get you out of my mind and that's why I came back to find you. I thought at the time that you must have been working for the hotel or the historical society. Something about you kept drawing me back. You see in my time this old hotel has changed many times. From the Casa Monica, to the Cordova, to the City of St. Augustine offices, and then refurbished and renamed the Casa Monica Hotel. But my main reason for coming was to find that beautiful young girl I saw a couple of months ago. Who smiled at this old man as though she knew me. You drew me back, just as though it was meant to be. I know this all must seem as though I have lost my mind, but it is the truth."

"Well, John, it is very strange to me, and also very hard to understand. First come over here. I want to show you something."

I walked over to her; she took me by the arm and turned me around.

"Now, John, look in that mirror and tell me what you see."

I looked up into the mirror, and there looking back at me was a young man in his mid to late twenties. He looked like me, but about forty years younger.

"John, does that look like a man in his late sixties?"

"No, it doesn't, but when I came here I was."

"John, I met you over a year ago. You were here writing a new book. We were introduced by my friends Mr. Weedman and Mr. Baya. Because I'm a school teacher, they thought we should know each other. I think I was a bit smitten by you and I thought you were with me."

"I was and I still am. On my first tour of the refurbished hotel I saw your picture hanging in the lobby. I didn't know then that we had met in the past, but to me it was a picture of the most beautiful girl I had ever seen. In that picture, you are looking directly into the camera with just a hint of a smile. It seemed as though you were looking at me, trying to tell me something. I knew then that I must find out more about this hotel and beautiful young lady. I researched all I could find on the hotel, but could find nothing on the picture. All anyone could tell me was that it was believed to be a local young lady, who was here right after the hotel opened in eighteen-eighty-eight. No one knew any more about her."

"John, I'm not sure that I believe or understand what is happening, but I want to know. If we are ever separated, go to the school house; I'll get word to you somehow."

"I'll remember that," I said. "I believe we, by some strange quirk of fate, are meant to be together." I held her close to me and kissed her gently. I felt a tingle go all through my body as I held her and we kissed; at the same time my heart seemed to almost skip a beat.

One day as we were walking the streets, I saw in the window a beautiful Greek Cameo. I knew at once that I must buy it for Dora. It would look great around her neck.

That evening we had dinner in the hotel dining room. After we had eaten, we saw that there was a photographer set up in the lobby, so I begged Dora to have her picture taken for me right then. As I saw her pose for the picture, I knew then that this was the picture I had seen in the hotel.

For the next few days we were together every day and as much of the day as possible. One afternoon, as the sun was going down, we sat on the rocks out by the old fort talking. I had my arm around her as we spoke.

"John," she said, "I do love you, but I'm afraid that this will all end at any moment. You will always be with me, won't you?"

I assured her that I would, and if I did ever return to my time, I would find a way to come back. I didn't know how, but I would somehow. That is, if she would not ever forget me. I'm sure that fate would not keep us apart. Fate brought us together and it would keep us together somehow. I just knew that it would.

Those past few days had been glorious for both of us. As the sun went down, Dora shivered a bit as it got cooler. I took my jacket off and placed it around her shoulders. Dora put her hand into one of the pockets and said, "What is this, John?" as she pulled her hand out and showed it to me.

I must have shown my shock, because Dora said, "What's wrong, John? You look like you have seen a ghost."

"I think I have. That's a nineteen-ninety-nine quarter, look at the date. That proves where I come from."

I held her very tightly as she said, "John, what's wrong? You look so pale."

I kissed her. "I think I'm going back!" I said, "Please remember me!"

I could hear her getting very faint.

"John, you're fading, I can see through you! Don't go, John, stay with me. I love you!"

"I'll be back Dora. I'll find a way! I'll find a way!"

As Dora faded away, I could see the tears flowing down her cheeks, as she kept calling to me. "John! John! Come back to me! I'll be waiting no matter how long!"

I awoke in my room at the Casa Monica as someone was knocking on the door.

"Mr. Rogero, you asked to be called for dinner."

"Yes. Thank you, I'll be right down."

I dressed and went down to the dining room. As I passed through the hotel lobby I couldn't help looking over on the corner wall near the back. There it was, among some other photos taken around the time of the hotel's grand opening. It was the picture I had had taken of her on that last night I had with her—around her neck was the cameo, just as it had been. I could see that beautiful half smile she had been able to hold while the photographer took the picture.

For the next few weeks I researched everywhere I could think of on Miss Dora Browne. I found that she had been a school teacher in St. Augustine in the 1880s, but after 1890 I could find nothing else on her, other than that she had moved away with no forwarding address.

About a month later, John Rogero's room at the Casa Monica was opened because he had not been seen for a few weeks and they were worried about him. As they looked around the room, all of his things were there and in order, but John was nowhere to be found. They found his journal on the table next to the window overlooking the park. He did most of his writing there as he watched the people below on the street and in the park.

His last entry in his journal was this: "I have researched all possible avenues to find a way to return to my Dora and at last I feel that I have found a way."

It was signed, John.

John was never seen again; some people say that he did find a way back. He found his beloved Dora, married her, and moved further south to become a wealthy landowner during Florida's first land boom. Others say that he found his beloved Dora at the Casa Monica, where they remain today. Some of the guests of the Casa Monica have inquired about the costumed couple they had met either on the stairway or in the old dining room. Everyone says the same thing, that they make such a beautiful couple, they look as if they truly could have stepped out of the 1880s, and they are always smiling.

21
The Ghost of the Light

St. Augustine

As the story goes, the ghost of the St. Augustine Lighthouse is the ghost of Lorina Alcontera. Lorina was about eighteen years old when she died. Some say that she killed herself by jumping off the lighthouse tower after hearing of the death of her beloved Roberto, who was killed by Indians over near Picolata on the St. Johns River. Others say that she died accidentally while trying to get away from Juan Valdez. It seemed that he had come to tell her about Roberto's death. Juan had always been in love with her, and some say that it was he, and not the Indians, who killed Roberto. When Juan made advances to her on the catwalk of the lighthouse tower, where Lorina was watching for Roberto, she slipped on the damp walk and fell to her death.

Juan left St. Augustine a few days later on a schooner that was headed for Havana. The schooner he was on never got there. No sign was ever found, except for a piece of wood that washed ashore a few weeks later. On the piece of wood was a message: "Our masts are all broken and we are taking on water. We see the light and are headed for it. Nearly all hands have been lost. I and a few of the crew are all that is left. It seems that we only have a short time left." It was signed "Juan."

No other sign of the schooner was ever found. There have been many stories and theories over the years as to what happened to it. One was that one of Florida's sudden storms came up and the schooner foundered, losing all on board. Another theory is that the ghost of Lorina directed the schooner's crew with the light onto a sandbar, where the storm broke the ship apart, and all other pieces of the ship were strewn up and down the coast. The most current theory is that the Bermuda (or Devil's) Triangle, which has claimed so many ships and people, claimed the schooner, too.

It has been more than 150 years since Lorina died on that warm, clear, fall night. There have been many people who believe that her ghost or spirit haunts the St. Augustine light. They claim to have seen her late on a clear night walking around the catwalk at the top of the lighthouse tower. There have been reports by ship crews who say they have seen a light coming from the general direction of the lighthouse, yet those ships were much farther out, and the crew should not have been able to see the light. Some say that it almost led them to destruction, others say that it saved them from running aground on a sandbar out on the snapper banks. Whoever or whatever it is, here are just a few of the stories that have been told of the Ghost of the St. Augustine Light.

One of the earliest recorded sightings of this well-known apparition was made in the lighthouse log book not long after the Civil War. Many tales have been told about it. The lighthouse keeper recorded the following:

"October 20, 1872. I have seen her again! I had lit the lamp on the light just before dark as usual. I had stayed up in the tower writing, and had completely forgotten the time and how dark it was getting. I spend quite a bit of time there because it's so peaceful and quiet. I can look out over the waters to the east and see the ocean. Look to the south and west, and see the Matanzas Inlet and the old Coquina quarries, or back to the north and have a beautiful view of St. Augustine.

I don't know how long I had been writing when I felt a cool breeze pass by. I looked out of the window. There standing by the rail on the catwalk was a young woman. The same one I had seen from the ground last month. She had long black hair that seemed to float down to below her waist. She was wearing a white dress. I stood and shouted to her. She turned to the door and stepped out onto the catwalk, just as she was turning around the corner. I called to her again and ran toward her. She was gone! I walked around and around the catwalk. I even looked down the stairs, but she was gone. Lorina didn't want to talk tonight!"

Another story takes place just at the turn of the century. Again it was October, this time in 1899. It seems that in St. Augustine, there had been a double murder of a young woman and her boyfriend by another man who was in love with her. The murderer had been chased by the sheriff and his men onto Anastasia Island, where they lost his trail. The sheriff and his men searched for him all night. Early the next morning, the lighthouse keeper was walking around looking things over for repairs because the light had been out for a few days. As the keeper came around the side of the tower, he saw what appeared to be a man curled up by some old coquina rocks. As he approached the man to tell him that he couldn't stay there, he saw that the man was badly hurt. The keeper called for some help to take the man inside, then he called for the doctor. The man was in very bad shape. While the keeper's wife cleaned off the man's wounds, the man, whom they learned was the one who had killed the couple in St. Augustine, told them what had happened. He had been hiding from the posse up on the light. He must have dozed off when he felt an unusual cool breeze. When his head cleared, there, standing directly in front of him, was a young woman in a long, white dress. She was pointing her finger at him but not saying anything. He jumped to his feet, knowing that he had been caught. As he backed up, the woman came toward him, still not saying anything. He stumbled and fell over the rail, and this is where he was found.

Before he died, he told the keeper that he had killed the girl and her boyfriend but that he hadn't meant to do it. He loved the girl, but she loved someone else. Her boyfriend came up and hit him in the face. He pulled out his knife and stabbed him in the chest. The girl started to scream, and he couldn't get her to stop. He held his hand over her mouth until she stopped screaming. He must have held it over her nose, too, because when he removed his hand, the girl was dead. He had smothered her to death.

It seems that justice was served after all, for many people say that

Lorina avenged these murders.

The next story of the light took place on November 11, 1917. The Great War, as they called it at that time, had been going on for quite some time across the ocean in France. Many young men had been killed and would never return to their loved ones back home.

That November morning, as the beach patrol made their rounds on the beach, they came across some wreckage, then some bodies. They found one German seaman still alive, and before he died, he told a strange story of the light.

The day before, their ship (or German Raider, as they were called) had sunk a ship off the coast, just off the mouth of the Matanzas River. The seaman was the quartermaster on this ship and was on the bridge when this very heavy rainstorm came up. After the storm passed, it became very foggy and dark. All of their navigational equipment went out. Then they saw the St. Augustine light. This was unusual because they should have been able to see the light long before they did. They took their bearings on the light and ran onto a sandbar. Not knowing that they were a German ship, one of their own submarines surfaced and blew them to pieces. After the seaman finished his story, he died.

The strangest thing about the seaman's story is that the St. Augustine light had not been on that night. In fact, it had not been on for months because of the war.

These are just three of the stories of the ghostly events at the St. Augustine light. There have been many stories because many people have seen the ghost over the years. She usually is seen walking around the catwalk at the top of the light. She is always wearing a long, white dress and is looking toward the northwest. This would have been the direction her young man would have come if he had returned at all. Those who have seen her up close say that she has the most intense stare, with the saddest eyes. Most say they don't really fear her, but feel more of a concern for her. The few who have been afraid and lived never seem to get over the apparition.

The old lighthouse, like so many of its kind, is no longer manned by a keeper. It is now all electric, and thus, fewer people are at the light at night. During the day, the old keeper's house is a museum and tours are taken around the place.

At the St. Augustine Lighthouse, many people climb to the top of the tower, where they have a beautiful view of Anastasia Island and Old St. Augustine off in the distance. They never know of this ghostly apparition that so many others have seen over the years. But should you be near the light some early fall night, look up at the catwalk on the lighthouse tower. You may see what could be a cloud or mist and feel a cool breeze pass you by, or you may see what appears to be a pretty young girl looking over the rails toward the northwest. If you do, you will know that Lorina is still there, walking the catwalk and watching for her lover to return. But beware if you are a person who has done something wrong—she may be looking for you.

22

The Lady in Pink

St. Augustine

The old Huguenot Cemetery is located just outside the old St. Augustine city gates and next to the Chamber of Commerce building. Many of the French Huguenots who are buried here died during the numerous outbreaks of yellow fever that plagued this area of Florida just before the turn of the twentieth century. The cemetery specter is seen now and then; the last sighting was less than a year ago, and a record of the earliest was found in the attic of the old schoolhouse.

The first was told by a schoolgirl in the 1850s. She handed in a paper at school telling about what she and her father saw when they came to town for supplies during the summer of 1851. She wrote:

My Pa and I had gotten our supplies in the wagon and were headed out the old gates past the cemetery to our place about a mile out of town. As we passed through the gates, we heard a scream coming from the cemetery. Pa pulled the wagon over to the side of the road and told me to stay in the wagon while he went to see if he could help. As we pulled over by the wall that ran around the cemetery, I saw what appeared to be a woman in her mid-twenties. She was dressed in a beautiful pink dress that seemed to flow around her. She was holding a handkerchief to her face and we could hear her crying.

Pa pulled out his pistol, just to be ready, then went through the gate towards the lady. Pa got within about thirty feet and I could hear him ask her if there was anything he could do. The lady in pink turned, looked him straight in the eyes and was gone. She had not run away, she had vanished right before our eyes. Pa stood there for a moment, then slowly walked back towards the wagon. We got almost home before he said a word. He then turned to me and said, "Elizabeth, did you see what I think I saw? Or have I gone crazy?"

"I saw it, Pa! How did she do that?"

There have been many reports of people hearing someone in the cemetery crying, but when they go inside, no one can be found. They continued to hear the crying, but it was heard in different places, thus making it hard to pinpoint. Wherever they go, the sobbing seemed to come from somewhere else.

Then, just a little over a year ago, a tourist was walking down the sidewalk with his wife, enjoying the city and their walk, when they heard crying coming from inside the cemetery. Thinking that someone needed help (they knew that no one had been buried in this cemetery for many years), they went inside. There in the back, next to the parking lot, they saw this young woman dressed in a pink lace dress. They reported that she had dark auburn hair with a deep scar on her forehead. Her dress was buttoned up high on her neck. She seemed to be in costume of an earlier time, about the late 1700s or early 1800s. She looked to be in her late twenties. They got within about ten feet of her before asking if they could help. All she said was, "Oh, my poor husband! Oh, my poor children!" Then she looked directly at them with tears streaming down her face and vanished right before their eyes. Startled, they ran from the cemetery, only speaking to the night clerk at their motel.

After the night clerk told the couple that this lady in pink had been seen by many people over the years, they decided to go by the St. Augustine Historical Society's office the next day to see if anything could be found out about her. After much research, they found that Maria Alonso Sanchez had lost her husband and two children to the Indians in the 1840s while coming to St. Augustine from Picolata, over on the St. Johns River. They had been attacked in their wagons by a small band of renegades. Her husband and two children, along with the wagon driver, were killed. Maria was shot with an arrow, scalped, and left for dead. Two days later she was found wandering down the road. Her family was buried in a plot just outside the old gates that is now the Huguenot Cemetery.

The paper said that for many years she could be found late in the afternoon crying beside their graves, always wearing pink, which was her husband's favorite color.

No one ever knew what became of her. The town always thought she was never just right in the head after the attack, and could understand why, so no one ever bothered her. After a number of years she just disappeared. They found a small slate lying on the graves which read, "I'll be here for you always." It was signed "Mama."

They searched the place where she lived, but no trace of her was ever found. The only thing that was missing was her pink dress. They couldn't find anything with her husband's or children's names on it, so a marker was placed on the gravesite which read, "Maria Alonso Sanchez, her husband and two small children. May they rest in peace, killed by Indians. (Also known as The Lady in Pink)."

23

The Quarry Pits

St. Augustine

For hundreds of years, coquina rock has been quarried from the pits on Anastasia Island, behind what is now the St. Augustine Alligator Farm. Coquina is formed in nature by the compacting of shells into stone. The rock has been mined for building many things from bridge foundations to homes, and most notably, the two forts—San Marcos and Matanzas—located in St. Augustine. This was a very useful rock for building forts in the old days because when ships or shore cannons fired a ball at the forts, the wall would more or less absorb the shot so it would not destroy the whole wall. Some of the walls of the forts were as much as fifteen feet thick. This made it nearly impossible to knock a hole in the walls.

No one knows how many tons of rock have been mined here. Originally, slaves and Indians under the Spanish rule mined it, and later it was mined by construction companies. The last company to mine this rock at the turn of the twentieth century was the North Florida Rock and Mining Company of St. Augustine. This story is about its last problem.

As the story goes, the company was doing very well in the 1890s when Henry Flagler started his construction in St. Augustine. He had many of his hotels and other buildings constructed of this rock since

The quarry pits, Anastasia Island, 2007

it would hold up under most weather conditions.

The rock mining had grown well into the island when the miners came upon an old Indian burial ground. The local Indians tried to tell them not to go any farther into this area or they would have trouble from the spirits. The mining company, though, was like many companies today in that they were only interested in money, so on they went mining the rock.

They hadn't been mining many weeks when things started to happen—small things at first. Their equipment started to break down for no apparent reason, but this didn't stop them from mining. People started having small job accidents, at first a hurt foot or a hand, then a broken arm or leg. Then one day it happened. The workers were loading some large stones into a flatbed truck when the rear end of the truck fell into a hole. The rocks slid off the truck, killing two of the workmen. The hole had not been there the day before. Coquina rock does not dissolve like limestone, so it couldn't have been a sinkhole that developed.

Nearly every day after that, someone got badly hurt. The workmen were becoming very uneasy and restless working there. The mining company hired a night watchman to stay there at night to prevent anyone from sabotaging the site.

The first night the watchman was at the site, he was given a pistol and a 30-30 carbine. When the crew came to work the next morning, they found the night watchman on the ground outside the shack, dead. His hair had turned completely gray and on his face he had a look of absolute horror. Both his rifle and pistol were completely empty. He was examined by the doctor, who found that he had been so frightened he had a heart attack and died.

The men at the site refused to work until something was done. The owners promised to place a crew of men out there to get to the bottom of this problem.

That night, five men were placed at the site. All were heavily armed. The next morning, all five men were found inside the workmen shack trembling with fear, crying, and totally frightened. Two were hysterical.

It was almost a week later that they had recovered enough to tell what had happened. Two of the men never got over the ordeal and ended up in a mental institution. James Walters finally got to the point where he could talk about it. His story follows.

We were doing fine before the sun went down. We had eaten our supper and were drinking coffee. Two of the men, Robert Adams and Hubert Wright, went out to make their rounds first. They weren't gone long when the rest of us heard yapping noises like a pack of dogs that had something treed. Bill Fenton went to the window and said, "My God, look!"

Sonny Ship and I ran to the window and looked out. Some Indians had Robert and Hubert tied to a stake torturing them. They were slicing at them with their knives. We could hear them scream and see the blood flow from their wounds.

Then they stopped screaming and the Indians started towards us in the shack. We fired over and over again, but they kept coming. It seemed nothing could stop them.

When we ran out of ammunition, we just huddled in the corner to wait for the death that we knew was coming. I have never been so afraid in my life. Had we not used up all our ammunition, we would have killed ourselves.

The next thing James remembered was the owner at the door. The owner checked the weapons, and indeed all had been fired until the ammunition was gone.

Robert Adams and Hubert Wright never recovered from the ordeal. Bill Fenton and Sonny Ship were never quite right and would not say a word about it. No one could tell us how Robert and Hubert got back to the shack, nor were they ever able to tell their story. The place was searched completely, but no Indians were found, other than those in the burial mounds.

The talk was that the ghosts of the Indians had stopped the construction and caused all the problems. If this is true, they accomplished what they set out to do, and that was to close the rock quarry. No more has been mined there since that time. James Walters did recover, but was never really the man he had been before that frightful night in the quarry pits.

You can still see where the rock was cut out of the old quarry site. Many homes have been built in the area around the Alligator Farm, and much of the quarry site is now a lake. I can't help wondering, though, why nothing has ever been built on the site of the quarry, since it could have been filled in and built on.

24

The Lady in Blue

St. Augustine

Henry Flagler, I would guess, has done more for the development of the east coast of Florida down to Key West than any other person. He made his home in St. Augustine and developed the Florida East Coast Railroad. He bought and built hotels, churches of many denominations, and buildings all over Florida, but more in St. Augustine than anywhere else. One of the grandest was the Ponce de Leon Hotel. At the time, it was considered one of the most modern and highest rated hotels in the United States, not only for its construction but its dining and other fine features. Its dining room, called the Tiffany Room, was and is very beautiful with its stained glass windows, all made by Tiffany.

Today, what was once the finest hotel in Florida and one of the grandest in the country is now the home of Flagler College, a private school. The Board of Accreditation rates it very highly for a small school. The conveniences it has today are still top-rated.

On the top floor of the college building, which is used as the housing area for the college's live-in students, the Tiffany Room is still used as a dining room, exclusively for the students. Others, though, see it on tours and visits to the college. The patio and grounds are still kept

in the same style and theme as when Flagler built it around the turn of the century.

This is the story of the lady dressed in blue at the hotel. Many people have seen her and even spoken to her at times. People who knew her say she was usually seen in the Tiffany dining room wearing a pale blue, lace dress with a wide-brimmed hat with flowers, white gloves, and white button shoes. She always sat at a rear table next to the window and ordered tea and cakes, never a full meal. She never spoke except when spoken to. She was reported to be in her mid- to late twenties and stunningly beautiful, but would never talk to prospective suitors or accept their invitations—that is, except for one time.

There have been many stories and theories about who she was and why she was there. But the one I like best is this one about her and Clifton A. Ward, a very close and respected friend of Henry Flagler who is mentioned in some of Flagler's old letters. Ward was also mentioned in his journals written in the 1890s: "We have received tragic news today, about Cliff's lady friend. I know how heartbroken he is because he had very strong feelings for her. He had even given up his present family to be with her. It's a real shame that she couldn't have waited a few days longer. Her beautiful face and blue silk lace have become a part of this hotel."

As the story goes, she had met Clifton Ward while on vacation in St. Augustine with her father, who was a U.S. Senator from Pennsylvania. Ward and this young lady became very close during her vacation. When she found that she was with child and told him, everything was fine until he told her that he had asked his wife for a divorce so he could marry her, but his wife had refused. When Ward told her this, she ran out of the dining room and up to her floor. As she reached the top, she slipped and fell down the stairs, breaking her neck. She was killed instantly. Ward, they say, went to pieces for a few weeks after her death. He then moved farther south. Some say he died a year or two later of yellow fever; others say that he died of a broken heart. His last words were "I'm coming, my blue bird, wait for me."

On the hotel register, there are many entries of guests who have seen the lady in blue on the top floor and at her regular table, as though she was waiting for someone. Some even mention seeing her with a handsome young man, both dressed in clothing of the 1890s. For years, the hotel kept her table marked, "Reserved for our Lady in Blue and her Guest."

Some of the students today tell of seeing her walk the halls at night. Sometimes they even get close enough to hear her sobbing for her lover and unborn child.

No one seems to understand why she still roams the halls and dining room, unless she and her Mr. Ward never got together and she is still waiting for him to return to her. Another version of the story is that Ward left her when he found out she was expecting a child and he never returned, and thus she was brokenhearted when she died.

Others say that the Blue Lady and Ward are together in the hotel where they had such happy times together, and that they are happiest there so they don't wish to leave as long as they are together.

Whatever the reason, those people who have spoken to her say she was always extremely polite and congenial. No one has ever reported a problem with her. Even some of the modern students at the college, if a cold breeze hits them in the halls or they see a mist, will tip their hats and say, "Have a nice day, Blue Lady," and go on about their business.

25

Castillo de San Marcos

St. Augustine

I first saw the ghost of Old St. Augustine's Castillo de San Marcos a year or so ago. This is not unusual, because I am sure with St. Augustine being the oldest city in America, I am not the first to have encountered a ghost in this old city.

Let me begin by going back a little. I have heard stories of ghosts, specters, and phantoms in the nation's oldest city, including stories about the Ghost of the Light, the Specters of Flagler College, the Specter of the Old Huguenot Cemetery, the Ghost of the Quarry Pits, and even some about the old fort. But the Ghost of the Castillo was my first encounter.

My wife and I love to visit St. Augustine to walk the streets, look at the sights, and explore the many shops. Every afternoon when we visited, we would walk down to the fort from our motel, which was about a block away on the waterfront. We would walk around the fort's moat, sometimes sitting on the sea wall and watching as the lights came on in the city harbor. It was a very relaxing time just to sit and wonder what the people here saw and felt hundreds of years ago.

One evening we sat on the sea wall until the sun went down. We started back to our motel, when we saw a flickering light coming from a small window next to one of the fireball ovens. The fort had been

closed to the public for quite some time that day. I pointed it out to my wife, but by the time she looked, it was gone. She said that it must be the night watchman or something. I agreed and put it out of my mind.

The next day I wanted to visit inside the old fort. I had been there many times, but something seemed to draw me more and more to it. My wife agreed to go, and upon entering, I asked the park ranger at the gate about the night watch at the fort. I got my first shock when he told me that they had not had a night watch inside the fort for over forty years—since World War II. I told him what I had seen the night before. He said that there must have been a reflection off some of the glass display cases as the lights came on. His explanation made sense to me, so I dropped the subject, but I still couldn't get it out of my mind. The light seemed more like candlelight than a reflection. As we were exploring, we found no display cases in the room where I had seen the light.

That evening, I decided to go back to the fort again. The sky was a little cloudy and looked like it might rain, so there were very few people out walking. I sat down on the old sea wall, again across from the fireball ovens, just looking out over the water. Then again I saw the flicker of light out of the corner of my eye. I turned and got quite a shock. There, coming around the side of the ovens, was a soldier carrying a lantern. He was dressed as a Spanish soldier of the eighteenth century and seemed to be looking for something. Then he turned, saw me standing there and started over towards me.

As he came closer, he spoke to me in Spanish. I had taken a little Castilian Spanish many years ago in high school, and though my Spanish wasn't very good, I remembered enough to tell him to speak in English. I was surprised that he spoke Castilian and not with a Cuban or South American accent. He told me he had been on patrol last night and had lost his family ring and was looking for it. He also told me that I had better go to my home because they had received reports that General Oglethorpe was coming to lay siege to the fort. With my English accent, I may be taken as a spy.

I was a little amused at first and thought this guy should be on stage. Many of the local people take part in special activities around town in full costume, but this guy was really great. If I hadn't known better, I would think he had stepped out of the early seventeen hundreds. We talked for a while longer and I even helped him look for the ring without success. He played his part to the very end. He seemed sincerely startled by any remarks I made on anything past the early seventeen hundreds, as if he thought I was crazy, or at least a little bit off. Finally he had to go in, so I decided to leave, too.

When I returned to my motel, I told my wife about my

encounter; she simply said that some people act out their parts all year and were very good at it.

"If you would like to," she suggested, "we could stop by the Castillo and report how good he was."

I thought that was a great idea because he should be praised, so the next morning after breakfast I drove by the park ranger's office. I reported my encounter and told the ranger I just wanted them to know how well this soldier played his part. The ranger looked at me for a moment, a little astonished, then said, "We have no soldiers playing the part at night. What did you say the man's name was?"

He seemed even more astonished at my answer. He reached into his desk and handed me a little booklet entitled "Unknown Facts about St. Augustine." Then he pointed to a page and paragraph and asked me to read it. I read, "On the night of the Oglethorpe siege of the Castillo, a Spanish officer was killed by Oglethorpe's first volley on the fort from Anastasia Island. Captain Don Carlos had been off duty watch and was out searching for a ring he had lost. The cannon ball caught him in the chest, killing him instantly. He was buried near the wall by the fireball ovens. It has been reported by many people claiming to have seen Don Carlos walk up and down by the ovens looking for his lost ring."

I returned to the car and told my wife what had happened. All she could say was, "Well, it looks as if you have made your first encounter with a real ghost."

I nodded and told her that she was probably right. I guess old Don Carlos will continue to search for his lost ring. I hope that someday he finds it.

26
Old Spanish Quarter
St. Augustine

The first time I heard of the specter in the Old Spanish Quarter was on the education channel on television. They gave a program on the ghosts in Jacksonville and surrounding areas, including St. Augustine. I had watched it and told my wife how well it was done. Then we passed it off as one of those things television stations do to attract listeners.

About a month later my wife and I went to St. Augustine just to look around as we so often do. We had seen just about everything there by this time, but we decided to visit the Old Spanish Quarter, which we had never visited before. I don't know why. It is a restored section of the original Spanish Quarter as it was in the early seventeen hundreds, and on the exact spot where it had originally been.

We started the tour just as all tourists would, going from one restored building to another and listening to each of the costumed actors as they presented their re-enactment of the place and times. In most cases I thought they were doing a very good job. When we came to the sergeant gunner's house the guide there really went into detail on each and every article about the old house. My wife and I were the only ones there at the time, so I guess she felt she could go into more detail. After her story, we began talking about our families. It seems

Governor's house patio, St. Augustine, 2007

that her family had been of Minorcan descent and had come over in the late seventeen hundreds. I told her that my people also came to Florida in the seventeen hundreds, but they were of English descent. They had been given land by King George of England over in Picolata on the St. Johns River. We talked for a while because it is getting quite unusual to find native Floridians nowadays, especially those whose family has been in Florida for so long.

After talking to her for a while, I asked if she had ever seen any ghost in the Quarter. I told her about seeing the program on television. She told me that she had not personally seen any, but many others had encountered unusual circumstances there at times. My wife and I then continued on with our tour.

After looking at the blacksmith shop and watching the smith make things much like they did long ago, my wife went over to look at one of the other buildings while I looked around the garden in back. As I was looking at how the people of that time had to really rough it by our standards today, I couldn't help wondering if I could have survived in that time. We just don't know how lucky we are today with all that we have. If it hadn't been for these great people, none of us would probably be here today. As I went from the old fire pit to the well, I happened to look up and see a beautiful lady sitting on one of the benches by an outdoor table. She looked to be in her early twenties and she wore a costume of the early Spanish period. Her dress was long and dark in color. She looked different from the others in the quarter I had seen. Their dresses had been rough and homespun, much as I would have expected of the people living in this area at that time. But this lady was different. She looked more aristocratic. She wore the dark dress with a lace shawl over her shoulders and a lace scarf over her head. She was just sitting there reading a book, not paying any attention to anyone around her. I thought to myself, no way could this lady have lived and worked outside like the others.

I walked over and spoke to her. "Hello. I was wondering, did many people dress as you do in the seventeen hundreds?"

She looked up at me then with the most beautiful dark eyes I had ever seen. "Were you speaking to me, señor?"

I thought I would go along with the play. "Why yes," I said, "do many people dress like you in this time?"

"Señor, I don't know who you are, but the answer would be yes and no. I happen to be here while Angela Sanchez finishes a dress she is making for me. I do not live in this area at all. And may I ask how an Englishman is allowed to walk around St. Augustine unescorted as you are? I know there is talk that Spain will sell the Floridas to England, but I didn't know that it had already been done. Now, if there are no other questions, I will continue reading while I wait for my new dress."

I thanked her for her time and information. As I walked over to catch up with my wife I couldn't help thinking that she did seem to be a bit haughty. But as I thought about it I realized that if there had been a lady of means here waiting for her dress to be made, she would most probably have been just like that. So as I left I said to myself that I would give her an A+ for her performance.

As I walked up to the next building to see what my wife was doing, she asked me where I had been. I told her that I had been over there by the well talking to that lady in black. My wife looked over and said, "I don't see anyone over there."

I looked, and sure enough she was gone. "Well, she was there just a moment ago."

"Sure," she said, "and I guess you'll tell me next that she was a ghost?"

"Well, maybe she was. Who knows?"

As we went out I asked at the gate about the lady in black, and was told that they only have people there who played the parts of those who lived here back then. I thanked them and told them how much we enjoyed the place, and how well everything was done.

In about a week or so my wife and I were touring the old Governor's house over on the plaza. We had talked many times about my encounter with the lady in black. My wife even teased me about making up a ghost just for her.

We walked from room to room in the Governor's house when my wife called to me. "Bob, come over here, you've got to see this."

My eyes followed her stare to the picture on the wall of the main room. There, as big as life, was my lady in black. She was dressed almost exactly as I had seen her in the garden in the old Spanish quarter.

"That's her!" I said. "That's the lady I spoke to the other day, the one I was telling you about."

"Sure it is," she said. "You've been here before and knew that you could describe the Governor's daughter."

"I swear to you, I have never seen this picture before. In fact I have never been in this building before."

I know she didn't believe me. If someone had told me a story like that, I don't think I would believe it either. But it's true—somehow I met the Governor's daughter in that garden that afternoon. I do hope before long I can go back there and see if I can meet her again. I have many more questions I would like to ask her about what it was truly like to live in St. Augustine in those days. We know quite a bit about how the average people lived, but not much about the aristocracy. But that would only be if she doesn't think I am too out of place in speaking to her.

Index

(Numbers in bold indicate photographs.)

Here are some other books from Pineapple Press on related topics. For a complete catalog, write to Pineapple Press, P.O. Box 3889, Sarasota, Florida 34230-3889, or call (800) 746-3275. Or visit our website at www.pineapplepress.com.

Florida's Ghostly Legends and Haunted Folklore Volume 1: South and Central Florida; Florida's Ghostly Legends and Haunted Folklore Volume 2: North Florida and St. Augustine; and *Florida's Ghostly Legends and Haunted Folklore Volume 3: The Gulf Coast and Pensacola* by Greg Jenkins. The history and legends behind a number of Florida's haunted locations, plus bone-chilling accounts taken from firsthand witnesses of spooky phenomena. Volume 1 locations include Key West's La Concha Hotel, the Everglades, Stetson University, and the Sunshine Skyway Bridge. Volume 2 locations include Silver Springs National Park, Flagler College, and the St. Augustine Lighthouse. Volume 3 covers the historic city of Pensacola and continues southward through the Tampa area, Sarasota, and Naples. (pb)

The Ghost Orchid Ghost and Other Tales from the Swamp by Doug Alderson. Florida's famous swamps—from the Everglades to Mosquito Lagoon to Tate's Hell—serve as fitting backdrops for these chilling original stories. Who but a naturalist can really scare you about what lurks in the swamp? Doug Alderson has been there and *knows*. From the Author's Notes at the end of each story, you can learn a thing or two about Florida's swamps, creatures, and history, along with storytelling tips. (pb)

Haunt Hunter's Guide to Florida by Joyce Elson Moore. Discover the general history and "haunt" history of numerous sites around the state where ghosts reside. (pb)

Haunting Sunshine by Jack Powell. Take a wild ride through the shadows of the Sunshine State in this collection of deliciously creepy stories of ghosts in the theaters, churches, and historic places of Florida. (pb)

Haunted Lighthouses and How to Find Them by George Steitz. The producer of the popular TV series *Haunted Lighthouses* takes you on a tour of America's most enchanting and mysterious lighthouses. (pb)

Ancient City Hauntings by Dave Lapham. In this sequel to *Ghosts of St. Augustine,* the author takes you on more quests for supernatural experiences through the dark, enduring streets of the Ancient City. Come visit the Oldest House, the Old Jail, Ripley's, the Oldest School House, all the many haunted B&Bs, and more. (pb)

Ghosts of St. Augustine by Dave Lapham. The unique and often turbulent history of America's oldest city is told in twenty-four spooky stories that cover four hundred years' worth of ghosts. (pb)

Oldest Ghosts by Karen Harvey. In St. Augustine (the oldest settlement in the New World), the ghost apparition are as intriguing as the city's history. (pb)

Best Ghost Tales of North Carolina, 2nd Edition, and *Best Ghost Tales of South Carolina* by Terrance Zepke. The actors of the Carolinas' past linger among the living in these thrilling collections of ghost tales. Use Zepke's tips to conduct your own ghost hunt. (pb)

Ghosts of the Carolina Coasts by Terrance Zepke. Thirty-two ghost stories from the coasts of the Carolinas that will make your hair stand on end. (pb)

Ghosts and Legends of the Carolina Coasts. More spine-chilling tales and fascinating legends from the coastal regions of North and South Carolina. (pb)

Ghosts of the Georgia Coast by Don Farrant. Here you will find plenty of evidence that the supernatural is alive and well in the Golden Isles of Georgia. Crumbling slave cabins, plantation homes, ancient forts—meet the ghosts that haunt Georgia's historic places. (pb)